Temperature's Rising
Galaxie 500

an oral history by
MIKE McGONIGAL

with a visual archive and commentary by
NAOMI YANG

20|20|20

Published by arrangement with Mike McGonigal and Naomi Yang

Originally published in 2012
by Verse Chorus Press for Yeti Publishing
as Yeti YB006

ISBN 978-1-7374400-1-7

Book design by Gregg Einhorn & Steve Connell
Thanks to Naomi Yang for her collection of images,
and to Shana McKenna for her expert scanning of them

Back cover photo by Michael Macioce
Inside cover: Detail from Johann Elert Bode's *Uranographia*, 1801
by permission of the Houghton Library, Harvard University
Frontispiece by R. Deluze, Paris, 1989

20-20-20
5 Brewster Street, Cambridge, MA 02138
www.20-20-20.com

Distributed by Artbook | D.A.P.
75 Broad Street, Suite 630
New York, NY 10004
www.artbook.com

Printed in Belgium by die Keure

Temperature's Rising
Galaxie 500

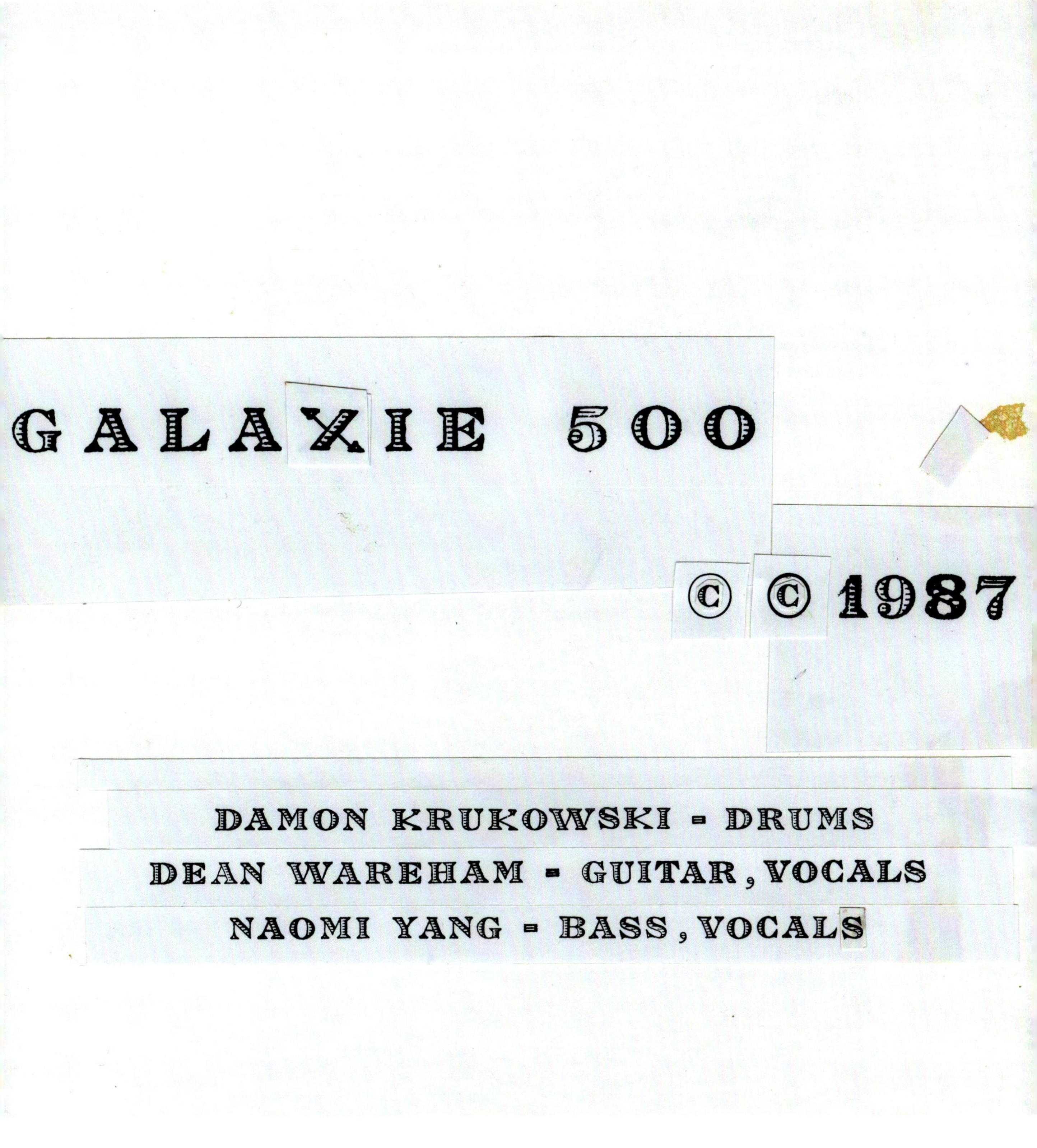

This is the mechanical (old-fashioned style graphic design) that I made for the typesetting of our first cassette in the summer of 1987. I was working at architect Aldo Rossi's office in New York City, and my boss received a beautiful engraved invitation to a wedding in Italy. I made a copy of the invitation and cut and pasted our cassette type together from it. There was no "X" and no "K" in the invitation so I had to make them up out of other letters and draw in the missing parts.

Summer 1987.

01 **BUZZ IN MY HEAD**

NAOMI YANG (*Galaxie 500 bassist*): I always think the band was like a movie star or a musician that died young—part of the mystique afterwards was that we never had a chance to grow old and for people to get bored of us.

MARC ALGHINI (*Aurora Records label head*): Music was going so fast and loud. Then Galaxie 500 came along, and it was so simple and basic that it was beautiful.

DAVE RICK (*Tour manager/occasional side guitarist*): They had a unique sound we were all excited to hear. Some of their influences were obvious, but what they were doing was clearly new and not just a reordering of ingredients. They didn't actually sound like anybody else. I continue to be amazed how knee-jerk and weak it was to label them, some sort of ersatz VU trip or rip—lazy and small-minded listening.

BYRON COLEY (*Writer*): In terms of Boston's general flow, they were almost an anti-band. But they were clearly working in a stylistic vein parallel to some of the things then emerging from the K or C86 anorak scenes. They just kept their boil level at a setting in line with the third Velvets LP, which was a good choice.

DAMON KRUKOWSKI (*Galaxie 500 drummer*): You know, we didn't play the way we did because we were trying to be different. It just came out that way.

KRAMER (*Galaxie 500 producer/"fourth member"*): To be perfectly honest, when they first came in and played for me, I thought, "these kids must be lying." There's no way they went to Harvard; they sounded so fucking retarded! One chord for an entire song? Played that slowly? Come on!

MARTIN ASTON (*Writer*): At the CMJ convention in New York City, autumn 1988, I was given a tiny fanzine praising a new rash of guitar-wave pop bands [including] Galaxie 500. Later that week, I got to see the trio play CBGBs Canteen. They somehow stitched together many of my favorites: the Velvets and '60s psych, Television, the Feelies, the Chills, Joy Division even (this was before they recorded "Ceremony")—and came sounding like new for those times: extraordinarily fragile, atmospheric, subdued, wild. I was totally in thrall to New Zealand pop at that time, and it fit perfectly. Out of place/time with what else was going on. Goosebumps all 'round.

SIMON RAYMONDE (*Cocteau Twins*): I used to stand on the side of the stage every night and watch the band, sometimes hypnotized by Naomi, struck by Damon's sensitivity as a drummer, but always enchanted by Dean's languid style of singing and playing.

DEAN WAREHAM (*Galaxie 500 singer/guitarist*): We didn't feel obscure or unloved, not by the standards of indie rock in the late '80s. Things happened pretty quickly for us; by the time *On Fire* came out we were very popular at college radio (which was important back then) and were embraced by the English music press too. I mean, we weren't as big as the Stone Roses, but I don't think we expected anything of the sort. Perhaps the fact that Rough Trade went out of business, and consequently the records were unobtainable for a few years, helped cultivate the mystique: if the records were out of print, then surely we must have been unloved.

CHRIS XEFOS (*Tour manager/sound guy*): They had a sound that really struck me, the whole slow, minimal, quiet and intense, but then sometimes loud, thing. Dean's New Zealand pedigree was a bit confusing but added an attraction since I was also part of the Flying Nun Lovers Club.

NORMAN VON HOLTZENDORFF (*Photographer*): What is most remarkable is how much I hear their sound and ideas in bands that came along later; they really tapped into something early on.

DAMON KRUKOWSKI: In the apartment Naomi and I [shared back then], we used to have an Ed Ruscha poster on the wall: "I Don't Want No Retrospective."

Poster artwork, Summer 1987.

Our first show, in Dean's apartment in NYC. My parents were architects and had a book of maps with every block/building in NYC in it. I found the page with Front St. and used it.

STUDIO DI ARCHITETTURA
45 W 17th STREET
NEW YORK, N.Y. 10011

MARIO DA POZZO E CHIARA DA POZZO

MEDA ANNUNCIANO IL MATRIMONIO

DEL FIGLYO GIOVANNI CON

VALERIA DE VECCHI

above **Part of the wedding invitation I used for the cassette typeface.**

below **The artwork for the cassette.**

Summer 1987.
Our first promo photo—taken on my camera by another high school friend in a "house" by Jean Dubuffet in East Hampton, Long Island.

Summer 1987.

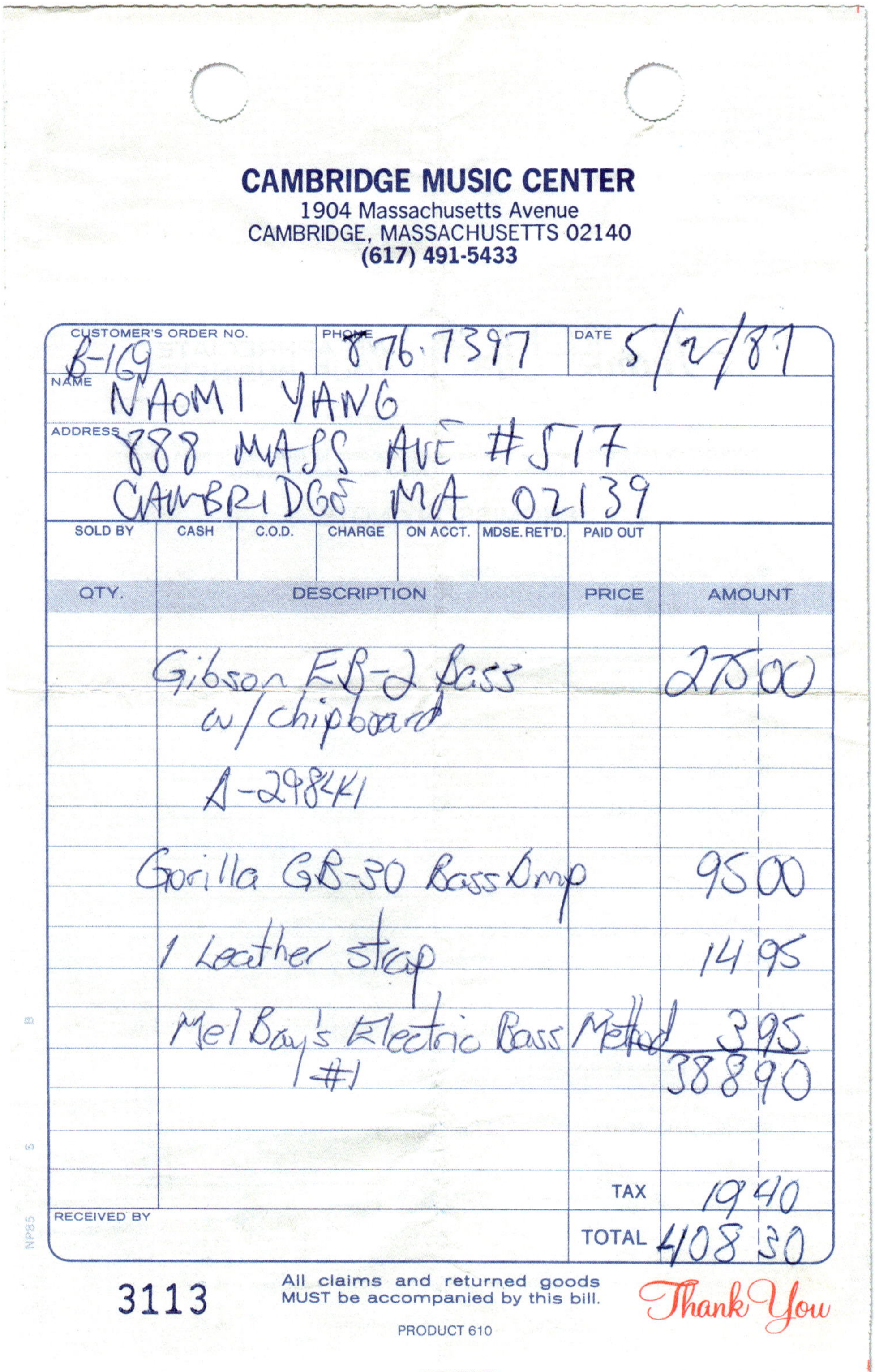

CAMBRIDGE MUSIC CENTER
1904 Massachusetts Avenue
CAMBRIDGE, MASSACHUSETTS 02140
(617) 491-5433

CUSTOMER'S ORDER NO. B-169 | PHONE 876-7397 | DATE 5/2/87

NAME NAOMI YANG

ADDRESS 888 MASS AVE #517
CAMBRIDGE MA 02139

SOLD BY	CASH	C.O.D.	CHARGE	ON ACCT.	MDSE. RET'D.	PAID OUT

QTY.	DESCRIPTION	PRICE	AMOUNT
	Gibson EB-2 Bass w/chipboard		275 00
	A-29841		
	Gorilla GB-30 Bass Amp		95 00
	1 Leather strap		14 95
	Mel Bay's Electric Bass Method #1		3 95
			388 90
		TAX	19 40
RECEIVED BY		TOTAL	408 30

3113

All claims and returned goods MUST be accompanied by this bill.

PRODUCT 610

Thank You

Receipt for the purchase of my bass, etc!

02 TEMPERATURE'S RISING

DAVE RICK: My young, exceedingly subjective impression was that they were "city kids" from the somewhat rarefied air of Manhattan. They met at private school; their parents did interesting things; they lived in interesting and/or swank nabes. In a old school and clichéd dichotomy out of Philip Roth, I felt like a loud, excited, less refined guy from Long Island. But, that was really just an invention—this was 1988, not '78, let alone '58 or '38. I'd enjoy whatever microscopic cultural or class difference I could muster. I'd play them some louder stuff, not that they hadn't heard the Stooges. And, I'm sure somebody was playing Zep in the Harvard dorms!

FRANCIS DIMENNO: They had a certain whiff of aristocratic hauteur. Of course, they all went to boarding schools and to Harvard. I did too, though I wasn't a legacy; I was a scholarship kid. Anyway, that's how I could recognize that whole ethos of "do anything, but whatever you do, don't make it look as though you're trying too hard." That's the default mode of jaded preppies the world over. It rubs a lot of regular people the wrong way. But if you're familiar with the code it doesn't bother you at all, because it's the standard operating procedure in that realm—particularly in academia.

DAMON KRUKOWSKI: We all went to the same high school on the upper east side of Manhattan.

NAOMI YANG: I met both Damon and Dean when I entered high school, in ninth grade, so that would have been 1978. They are both a year older and were cool tenth graders. Dean and I were in the same homeroom, and Damon's oldest friend was also in the same homeroom, so Damon would stop by a lot. But it was a small school, so you pretty much knew everyone.

DEAN WAREHAM: I met Damon in my ninth grade history class. He borrowed my notebook when he missed a few classes due to illness. And then he lost it. Damon was very kind; he always laughed at my jokes, even if they weren't funny. We remained friendly throughout high school and acted in a couple of plays together.

DAMON KRUKOWSKI: Naomi and I grew up ten blocks from one another, and actually went to the same school from kindergarten on, but we are a year apart so we weren't really aware of each other till high school.

NAOMI YANG: As high school went on, we kind of all hung out with the same group of people—the ones who were interested in listening to punk rock music and also the people who participated in the school theater. Damon and Dean were both acting—I was designing posters and sets.

DAMON KRUKOWSKI: It was a school that valued arts more than sports, so her skill always earned her a lot of respect. We started dating the spring of my senior year.

DEAN WAREHAM: Naomi was a year behind us in high school, but I took one class together with her and we were friendly even then; she was a really lovely person. I got to know her much better after she started dating Damon—but this would have been after I graduated high school.

DAMON KRUKOWSKI: Dean and I are the same age. His family moved [from New Zealand] to New York our freshman year of high school. I remember we took European history together that fall from a woman who was having an affair with another teacher, a leftist who would come and harangue our class from time to time as a part of their flirtation. So I think our political consciousness was raised simultaneously. Our circles in high school were different, but overlapped.

After graduation, we entered Harvard together and started hanging out more then. Music and politics were shared interests from the start. In college I joined the socialists, and Dean joined the communists. I think we may have been the only ones in those two groups who hung out together! And we started a band.

DEAN WAREHAM: Damon and I really became friends when we went off to college, and formed our band, Speedy & the Castanets.

DAMON KRUKOWSKI: "Speedy & the Castanets"? That seemed clever at the time!

DEAN WAREHAM: I'm going to credit our bass player, Marc Glimcher, [for the name], but I could be wrong. I know he bought the castanets because he paid for all our instruments.

NAOMI YANG: I wasn't in Speedy & the Castanets. Damon and Dean and Marc (another friend from our high school) started it when they were all freshmen at Harvard. I was still in high school. But the next year I attended Harvard too, and that's when I decided they needed a logo for the band as well a backdrop when they performed. I made them a backdrop out of a sheet that I spray-painted with the logo. It looked cool, but I don't think added anything to their success.

DAMON KRUKOWSKI: Naomi came to Harvard the next year, and a couple of years later she and I moved off campus to live together.

NAOMI YANG: Later, Marc quit Speedy & the Castanets and we all graduated. It was after college, when I was in my first year of architecture school, and miserable, that Damon and Dean started talking about reforming a band. I thought that sounded like fun and volunteered to play bass.

DAMON KRUKOWSKI: When Naomi joined, all the things Dean and I had been trying to do started to work.

NAOMI YANG: I had been listening obsessively to Joy Division and had been realizing that my favorite parts were always the bass lines.

DAMON KRUKOWSKI: People used to call bands on our scene "college rock," but we were older than that when we started recording.

Speedy & the Castanets

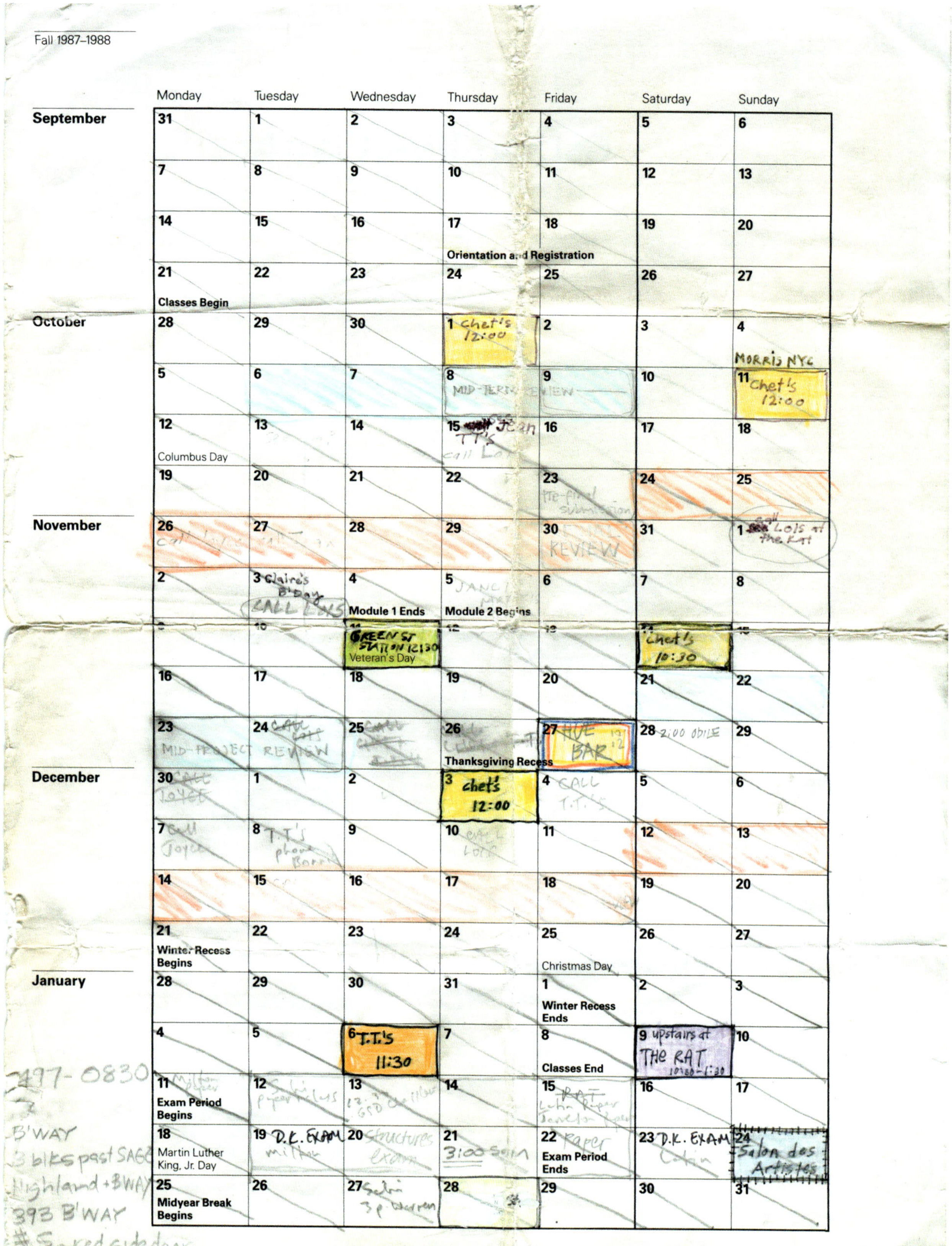

Graduate School of Design calendar, Fall 1987–Spring 1988.
My official school calendar, covered with gig information. I was more interested in the band than architecture school.

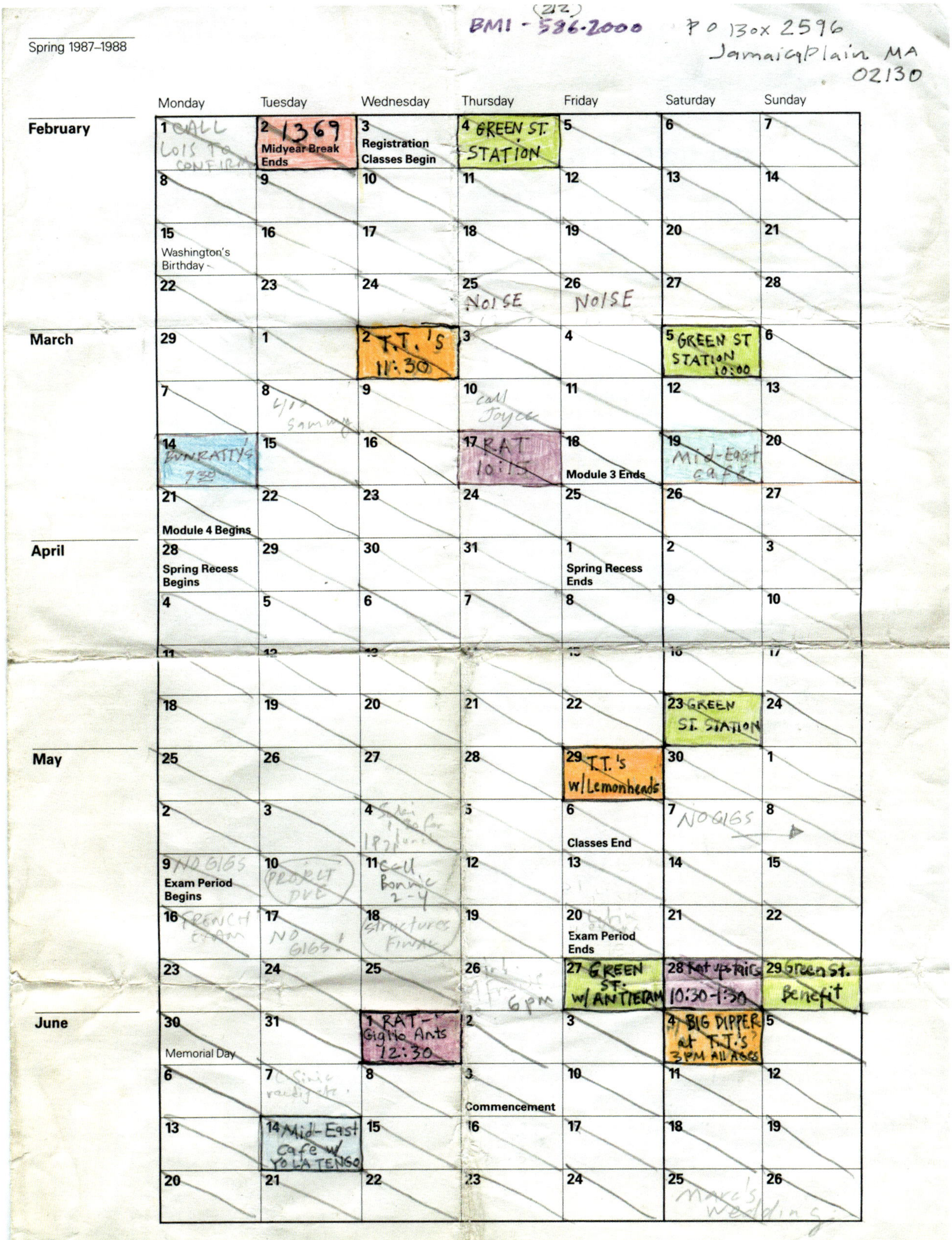

Spring 1987–1988

BMI - (212) 586-2000

PO Box 2596
Jamaica Plain MA
02130

	Monday	Tuesday	Wednesday	Thursday	Friday	Saturday	Sunday
February	1 CALL LOIS TO CONFIRM	2 1369 Midyear Break Ends	3 Registration Classes Begin	4 GREEN ST. STATION	5	6	7
	8	9	10	11	12	13	14
	15 Washington's Birthday	16	17	18	19	20	21
	22	23	24	25 NOISE	26 NOISE	27	28
March	29	1	2 T.T.'S 11:30	3	4	5 GREEN ST STATION 10:00	6
	7	8	9	10 call Joyce	11	12	13
	14 BUNRATTY'S 7:30	15	16	17 RAT 10:15	18 Module 3 Ends	19 Mid-East cafe	20
	21 Module 4 Begins	22	23	24	25	26	27
April	28 Spring Recess Begins	29	30	31	1 Spring Recess Ends	2	3
	4	5	6	7	8	9	10
	11	12	13	14	15	16	17
	18	19	20	21	22	23 GREEN ST. STATION	24
May	25	26	27	28	29 T.T.'s w/Lemonheads	30	1
	2	3	4	5	6 Classes End	7 NO GIGS	8
	9 NO GIGS Exam Period Begins	10 PROJECT DUE	11 call Bonnie 2-4	12	13	14	15
	16 FRENCH EXAM	17 NO GIGS!	18 structures FINAL	19	20 Exam Period Ends	21	22
	23	24	25	26 6pm	27 GREEN ST. w/ ANTIETAM	28 Rat upstairs 10:30-1:30	29 Green St. Benefit
June	30 Memorial Day	31	1 RAT - Giglio Ants 12:30	2	3	4 BIG DIPPER at T.T.'s 3PM ALL AGES	5
	6	7	8	9 Commencement	10	11	12
	13	14 Mid-East cafe w/ YO LA TENGO	15	16	17	18	19
	20	21	22	23	24	25 Marc's Wedding	26

Dean Wareham
GALAXIE 500
32 Adrian St., #2
Somerville, MA 02143
(617) 623-2441
(617) 876-7397

Dear :

I'm writing on behalf of GALAXIE 500. We're a three-piece (Naomi Yang on bass and vocals, Damon Krukowski on drums, and Dean Wareham on guitar) currently playing in Boston. We went to high school together in New York, then to college at Harvard where we learned a few guitar chords and drum-beats.

We recorded this demo-tape on an 8-track at 6/8 studios in New York this past summer. We like the songs but aren't as happy as could be with the overall sound because it's a little too clean.

We like some of the bands on your record label and thought you might be interested in helping us out with an EP, or a single, or an album. We've got lots of groovy new material and know we could sound beautiful with the right production.

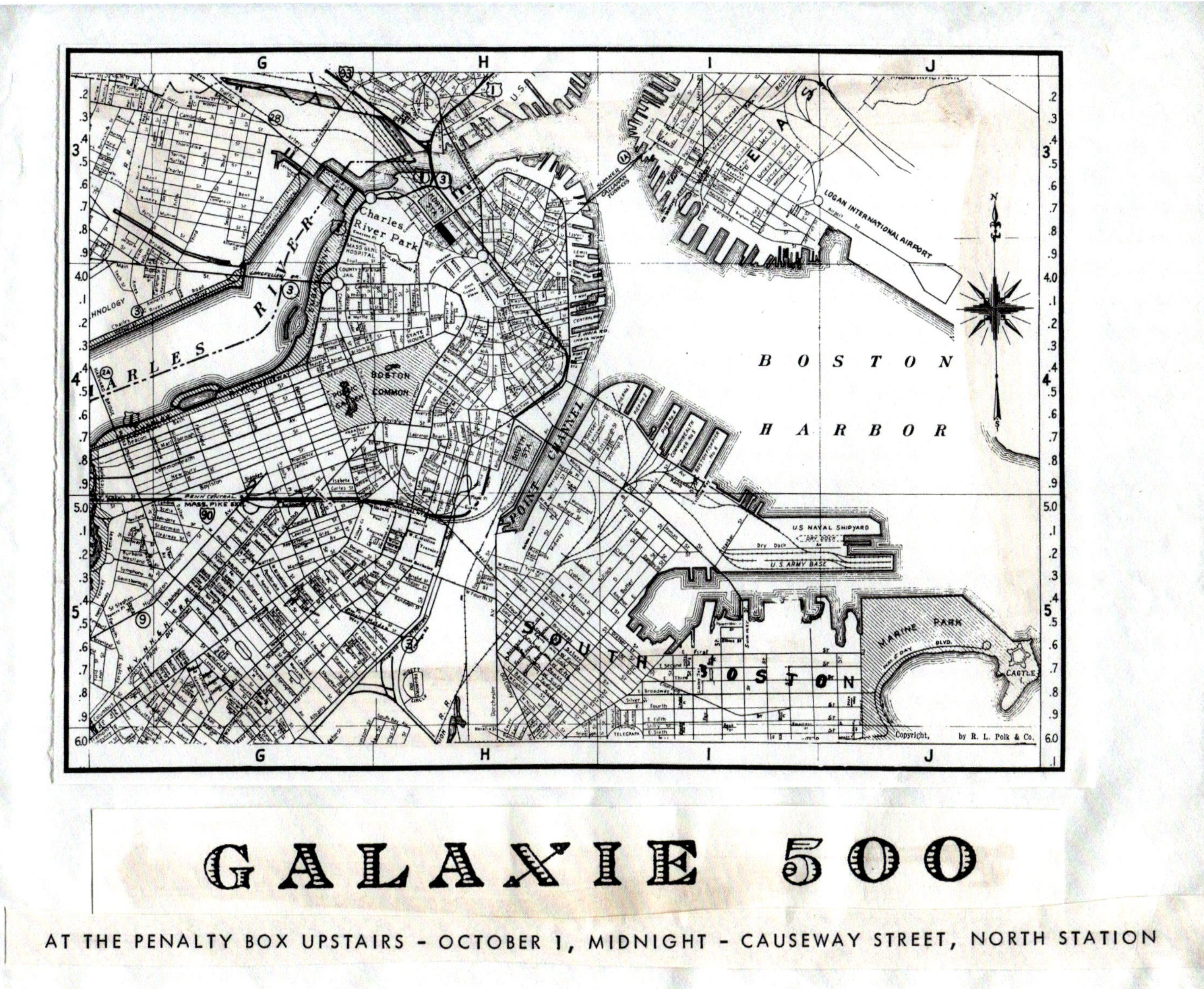

Poster artwork, Fall 1987.
Chet's Last Call, upstairs from the The Penalty Box bar, was the first club that booked us in Boston—but they booked anyone—all you had to do was call. It was across the street from the old Boston Garden and was a part-time rock club, part-time strip bar, and a full-time mysterious place.

Chet's Last Call, Fall 1987.
Photos by Sergio Huidor, who later directed all our music videos.

Chet's Last Call, Fall 1987.

Poster artwork, Fall 1987.

Chet's Last Call, Fall 1987.
We actually used this as a promo photo. Photo by Sergio Huidor.

The view from our rehearsal space, which was in an old loft building in Boston's South End. It overlooked the highway and the wholesale flower market. I always liked that the building across the street had the number "500" on it.

Poster and artwork for tickets, Spring 1988.
For local shows, you had to have your friends bring tickets with them to show the club how many people your band brought in. I took it as another opportunity to make ephemera. I used an old IBM "Executive" typewriter to do the typesetting—it was a special machine—the font was Futura!

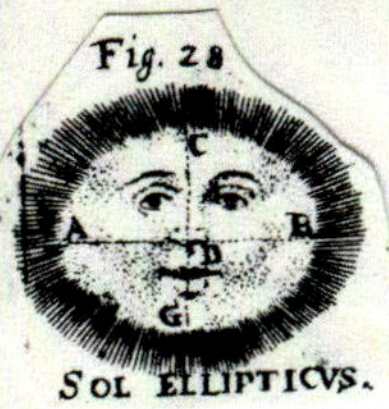

GALAXIE 500

Wednesday, March 2, 1988 - 11:00 p.m.
T.T. THE BEAR'S PLACE 10 Brookline St.
Central Square, Cambridge 492 - 0082
PLEASE BRING TICKET

GALAXIE 500

Wednesday, March 2, 1988 - 11:00 p.m.
T.T. THE BEAR'S PLACE 10 Brookline St.
Central Square, Cambridge 492 - 0082
PLEASE BRING TICKET

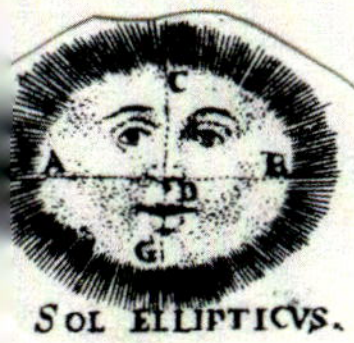

GALAXIE 500

Wednesday, March 2, 1988 - 11:00 p.m.
T.T. THE BEAR'S PLACE 10 Brookline St.
Central Square, Cambridge 492 - 0082
PLEASE BRING TICKET

GALAXIE 500

Wednesday, March 2, 1988 - 11:00 p.m.
T.T. THE BEAR'S PLACE 10 Brookline St.
Central Square, Cambridge 492 - 0082
PLEASE BRING TICKET

GALAXIE 500

Wednesday, March 2, 1988 - 11:00 p.m.
T.T. THE BEAR'S PLACE 10 Brookline St.
Central Square, Cambridge 492 - 0082
PLEASE BRING TICKET

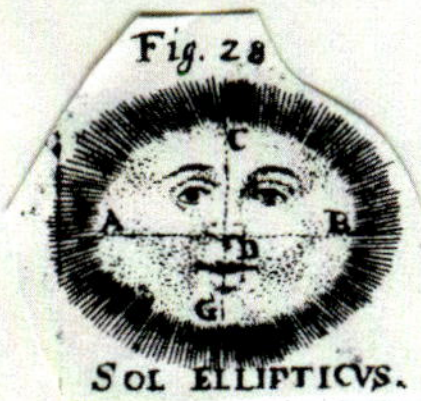

GALAXIE 500

Wednesday, March 2, 1988 - 11:00 p.m.
T.T. THE BEAR'S PLACE 10 Brookline St.
Central Square, Cambridge 492 - 0082
PLEASE BRING TICKET

GALAXIE 500

Wednesday, March 2, 1988 - 11:00 p.m.
T.T. THE BEAR'S PLACE 10 Brookline St.
Central Square, Cambridge 492 - 0082
PLEASE BRING TICKET

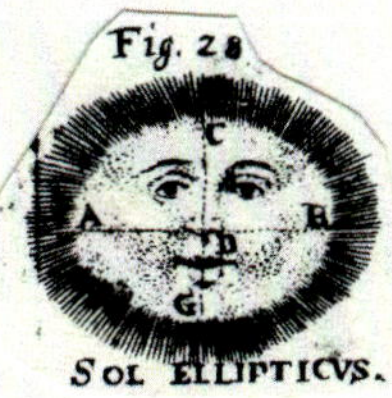

GALAXIE 500

Wednesday, March 2, 1988 - 11:00 p.m.
T.T. THE BEAR'S PLACE 10 Brookline St.
Central Square, Cambridge 492 - 0082
PLEASE BRING TICKET

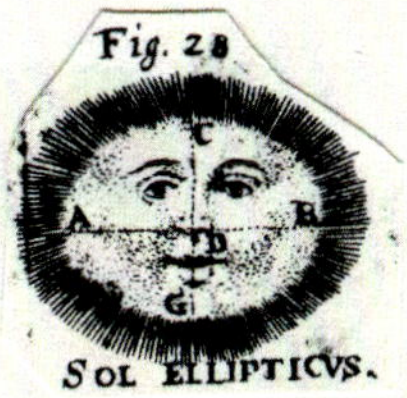

GALAXIE 500

Wednesday, March 2, 1988 - 11:00 p.m.
T.T. THE BEAR'S PLACE 10 Brookline St.
Central Square, Cambridge 492 - 0082
PLEASE BRING TICKET

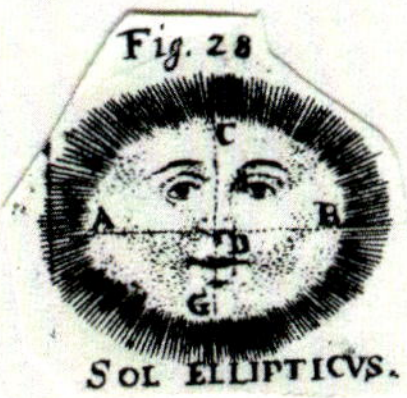

GALAXIE 500

Wednesday, March 2, 1988 - 11:00 p.m.
T.T. THE BEAR'S PLACE 10 Brookline St.
Central Square, Cambridge 492 - 0082
PLEASE BRING TICKET

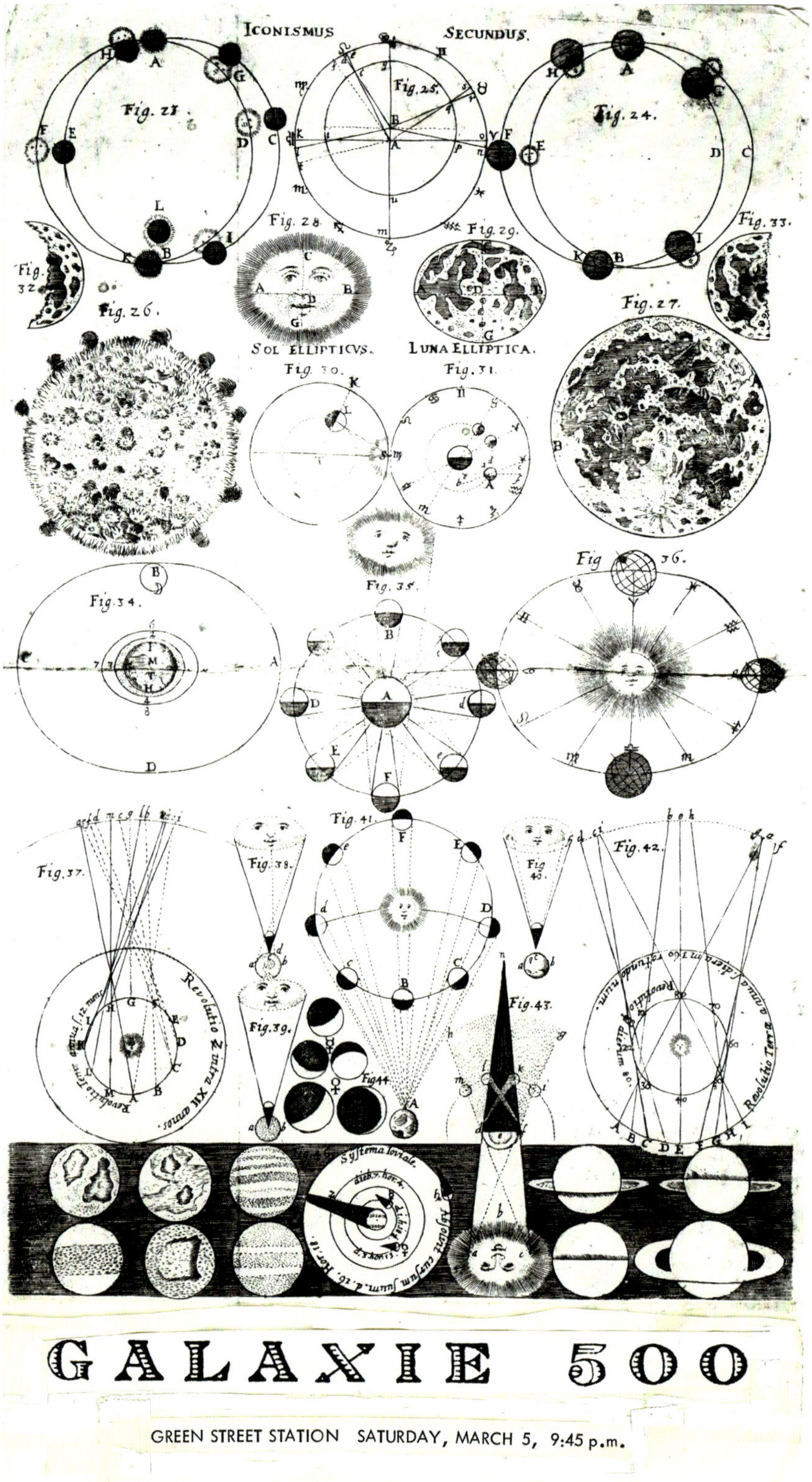

Poster artwork, Spring 1988.

Green Street Station, Jamaica Plain, Spring 1988.

Green Street Station, Jamaica Plain, Spring 1988.

REMO
Galaxie

wmbr
88.1fm
3 Ames Street
Cambridge
Massachusetts
02142
Telephone
617-253-4000

Jeff Parker, Music Director
Compiled by David Greene

ROCK PLAYLIST FOR APRIL 1988

ALBUMS

	Artist	Title	Label
1.	Naked Raygun	Jettison	Caroline
2.	Didjits	Hey Judester	Touch and G
3.	All	Allroy Sez	Cruz
4.	Butthole Surfers	Hairway to Steven	Touch and G
5.	Salem 66	Natural Disasters...	Homestead
6.	Sloth	LP	Soundwork
7.	Outnumbered	Work, Buy, Die	Edible
8.	Dredd Foole and the Din	Take off Your Skin	PVC
9.	Phantom Tollbooth	Power Toy	Homestead
10.	Union Carbide Productions	In the Air Tonight	Radium
11.	Rifle Sport	White:Made in France	Ruthless
12.	Pixies	Surfer Rosa	4AD/Rough T
13.	Howling Dogs	Rock On Ringo...	Downkiddie
14.	Pere Ubu	Tenement Year	Fontana
15.	Zodiac Mindwarp	Tattooed Beat Messiah	Vertigo
16.	Moral Crux	LP	Velvetone
17.	Sister Double Happiness	LP	SST
18.	Venom	Calm Before the Storm	AJK
19.	Sex Pistols	Live	Restless
20.	Verbal Assault	Trial	Giant
21.	The Fall	Frenz	RCA
22.	Blissed Out Fatalists	LP	Motiv
23.	X	Live at Whiskey A Go Go	Elektra
24.	Thin White Rope	In the Spanish Cave	Frontier
25.	Gibson Brothers	Big Pine Boogie	Okra

EP's, 45's & TAPES

	Artist	Title	Label
1.	Anastasia Scramed	What Kind of Truth Is This	PDI 7"
2.	Nova Mob	Cavalry/Madhouse	Novahoe 7"
3.	Buffalo Tom	Sunflower Suit	Local Tape
4.	Blood Oranges	Shady Grove	Local Tape
5.	Busted Statues	Silence	Local Tape
6.	What Now	Big Rock	Local Tape
7.	Hullabaloo	It's Not Enough To Play Loud.	Godawful EP
8.	Tall Paul	Mainline	Local Tape
9.	Lucky Pierre	Communique	Banana EP
10.	Galaxie 500	Tugboat	Local Tape
11.	God	My Pal	Au Go Go 7"
12.	Das Damen	Reverse Into Tomorrow/Bug	SST 7"
13.	Soul Asylum	Sometime To Return	A & M 12"
14.	Cryptones	Where'd She Go	Local Tape
15.	Things That Aren't Food	Jimmy	Local Tape
16.	The Roys	Ain't A Pretty World	Local Tape
17.	Condo Pygmies	Breathe Red	Local Tape
18.	Red Wagon	Deception	Local Tape
19.	Firehose	Sometimes	SST EP
20.	Vaselines	Dying For It	53rd & 3rd E

MARTIN ASTON: They played slow when everyone was fast. They were defiantly lo-fi before it became accepted, they preceded shoegazing, but never felt as posy as much of what followed. It was totally out of time, not in a scene, music that existed because they just felt like playing it, or were limited by how they played. Punk mentality. "We're aspiring to primitivism," Damon once told me.

NORMAN VON HOLTZENDORFF: I met the band at Harvard (through Sergio Huidor, who later did their videos). I went to one of their first gigs at a dive bar in Jamaica Plain, MA in the mid '80s. I vaguely remember carrying some equipment, so I think I can claim to be one of their original roadies!

FRANCIS DIMENNO: I can't be 100 per cent sure I was actually the first person to write about the band. But [Dean is] pretty media-savvy, and if he says I was, then perhaps it's true. Damon or Dean suggested I go see them at T.T. the Bear's at a January 6, 1988 gig, which I did. It wasn't much of a stretch for me. At the time I lived over Hi-Fi Pizza—literally three doors down from T.T. the Bears. I liked them very much, and predicted they would be big. It surprised me when my prediction actually seemed to be coming true.

BYRON COLEY: Pretty sure I saw their earliest shows that were held not at Harvard. I can't recall who first mentioned them, but they were very cool and minimal right from the start, a bit in the Young Marble Giants vein, which was real different than most Boston stuff at the time.

JOYCE LINEHAN (*Booker*): I do think I booked one of their first shows at Green Street Station in Jamaica Plain, and I did love the band dearly!

FRANCIS DIMENNO: They reminded me very much of what was known as the Hoboken sound: the Feelies, Yo La Tengo; and also, to a certain extent, the Athens sound—not so much R.E.M., more like some of the more contrarian groups, like Pylon or Time Toy.

NORMAN VON HOLTZENDORFF: The surprise is actually how much their sound was a harbinger of other sounds to come.

BYRON COLEY: I liked the impression they gave that they were amateurs, striving for something beyond their technical reach. They were not very well regarded in their home town when they were around. College DJs loved them, but they kinda got swamped in the Pixies/Throwing Muses/Lemonheads gush of that period.

MARC ALGHINI: I was at Taang!; I started working there while I was still in college in the mid-'80s. I was the first employee for the label, when they first put out the Lemonheads and Gang Green records—it was all just starting to blow up. I worked on the Mission of Burma record. Galaxie 500 had sent a tape to Curtis, the label's owner. He didn't really get it; Boston was like metal at the time, all the hardcore was super loud and getting to sound more like metal. Then there was this tape from this weird band. I called them and said, "You're wasting your money sending it to record labels like this."

FRANCIS DIMENNO: It was very clear to me that all three were very cerebral. Boston is a fairly cerebral city, of course, but of all the musicians I've interviewed—and I've probably interviewed well over 200—few of them had anywhere near the sheer brain power of Damon. Dean gave less of an impression of being whip-smart, and more of an impression of being really wired into the New York social scene.

DEBORAH ORR (*Writer*): The thing I most remember from back then is that Marc, who put out their first record, was such a total believer in the band and was running their label on a shoestring, if that.

MARC ALGHINI: They said they were going to record some songs with Kramer. So, I thought, maybe I could start a label. I figured I could run it at the same time that I was working with Curtis. So I gave them the money to go work with Kramer.

DEAN WAREHAM: Kramer was not a big name producer; Robert Christgau called him "pseudo-legendary." I was familiar with Shockabilly, who I had seen live at a New York club called 8BC. But it was probably the Half Japanese album he produced—*Music to Strip By*—that was the impetus.

NAOMI YANG: Dean read an interview with Kramer in a fanzine that said he did production work for hire. I think we just called him up. We wanted an alternative to the studio in Boston where everyone was going at the time. We didn't really identify with that sound, and all three of us felt more tied to New York. So it felt perfectly natural and a more interesting idea to go there to record.

DAMON KRUKOWSKI: We had been listening to a Half Japanese record produced at Noise, "US teens are spoiled bums! US teens are spoiled bums!"—it sounded very spacious. All the other Boston bands were recording at the same studios in town, which were turning out a very heavy, dense sound, like the Volcano Suns. Peter Prescott is a drumming hero of mine; I've always loved the way he makes his kit sound, but we were looking for something else. We weren't a heavy band, after all. We called to ask the rates. They were cheap! So we booked time. That's how we came to record the "Tugboat" single at [his studio] Noise, and how we met Kramer. It turned out he was the only employee.

The "Tugboat" 7" sleeve, 1988.

The "Tugboat" 7" sleeve (back).

KRAMER: I got a call from Damon out of the blue saying he was a musician from Harvard and don't hold it against him, and he asked me if I could get that drum sound from *Music to Strip By*. I lied and said sure, come on down. I was still learning my craft but I wasn't going to say will you bring the same drum set with you? They came down and they walked in the door and none of them were smiling; it seemed like something terrible had happened beforehand. I actually wondered if they'd broken up beforehand and just decided to keep the date anyway since they'd booked it. Later I found out they were terribly nervous and didn't know what to say.

DEAN WAREHAM: [My favorite memory of the group is] when we left Noise New York for the first time. We had three songs that we were actually proud of: "Tugboat" and "King of Spain," which became our first single, and "Oblivious," which we gave to that Chemical Imbalance fanzine, which included a 7" single in each issue.

MARC ALGHINI: It all just came together for the "Tugboat" single. I used Nashville Record Pressing; all the punk labels used them so I did it down there. But I was like a marketing and promotions guy—definitely not a label owner. It was that DIY thing, where you flew by on the seat of your pants. I literally had no idea what I was doing with Galaxie 500. I knew you gotta get records in the stores and get the band in a van and on the road, even if the show is just for ten bucks and a slice of pizza.

FRANCIS DIMENNO: Jeffrey Gagnon (aka J. Gags) of the Well Babys and I collaborated on quite a few songs, and one of them, "Be Kind," ended up being recorded by Kramer. So, I know from personal experience that Kramer could take what is essentially a fragment or an idea for a song and turn it into a full-blown production. I think that's what he did with "Tugboat," which, in a peculiar way, really nailed the zeitgeist of that particular time. The song was like the all-purpose response "whatever," long before "whatever" became a cliché. People on the East coast, particularly in Massachusetts, were getting all worked up over the coming Bush vs. Dukakis election. What direction was the country heading? Would it be four more years of Reaganism, or a return to technocratic Carterism, with an obscure Governor from a small state once again running the country? Dean, who was born in New Zealand, was detached from all that. He claims in his book that he wrote the song during that infamous January 6, 1988 after-party at the Meltdown house. In the interview [I did with them at the time], however, he actually claimed that he wrote the lyrics for it "in ten minutes, in the studio." Whatever! Again, it's that tossed-off, don't-care-too-much attitude in play.

DAVE RICK: I was the ersatz road manager and roadie on their first tour. I'm guessing it was in support of their first single. It might have been only a week-long tour. Most of the gigs were played in front of five people. Clearly these were people with their ears to the ground, fanzine readers and writers, friends of whatever brave soul put a show together, early Shimmy-Disc acolytes. I remember having fun.

DAMON KRUKOWSKI: It was an adventure from the start. I think every band experiences that same thrill—it's like joining the circus.

Nashville Record Productions
469 CHESTNUT STREET
NASHVILLE, TENNESSEE 37203
PHONE 259-4200

Invoice

No. A 64723

Date 5-11-88

Your Order No.

Shipped to

Sold To DAMON KRUKOWSKI
GALAXIE 500
888 MASS.AVE, APT 517
CAMBRIDGE, MA 02139

Our Order No.	Salesman	Terms	F.O.B.	Date Shipped	Shipped VIA

Quantity Ordered	Quantity Shipped	Stock Number/Description	Unit Price	Unit	Amount
		NR 17427			
		1000-7" RECORDS (LP)	632.00		
		PRINTED SLEEVES(DIFFERENT COLOR ON EACH SIDE)	155.00		
		BLUE VINYL	90.00		
		7" D/F REFERENCE	30.00		
		PMS INL ON COLOR	38.00		
		UPS	40.22		
					980.22
		PRE PAID 500.00			

This Invoice is due 10th of month following date of invoice. A service charge of 1½% will be added to any unpaid balance after 30 days. Collection charges will also be added if any are incurred. Not responsible for parts and labels after 1 year.

WilsonJones
GRAYLINE FORM 44-411 3-PART
©1983 • PRINTED IN U.S.A.

Original / Invoice
86

Receipt for pressing of the "Tugboat" single, Spring 1988.

The arrival and numbering of our first single, May 1988.
Taken in Damon's and my old apartment on Mass. Ave., with Marc Alghini of Aurora Records.

▲ **Flyer, Spring 1988.**
Helldorado was run by Billy Ruane, a legendary Boston music fan of boundless energy and enthusiam who danced wildly at every show.

▶ **First interview, *The Noise*, Summer 1988.**

GALAXIE 500

PHOTO: MARC GILMCHER courtesy Pace/MacGill

GALAXIE 500 or I JUST WANT TO BE YOUR TUGBOAT CAPTAIN

BY FRANCIS DIMENNO

On May 25th Galaxie 500 sat on my rooftop, eating a pepperoni pizza, swilling coke and talking about J. Richman. Naomi, the bass player, described how Dean had attended a recent performance at Nightstage and requested "Affection", and Richman wouldn't do it. "He said, 'Just because somebody has the loudest voice doesn't mean they always get their way.'" Damon, the drummer, suggested that these were words to live by. Words which describe the live sound of this intriguing trio: jangle without rasp, tangle without snarl, fluidity and ease without a gram of dull drone. Both sides of their first single, "Tugboat"/"King of Spain", recorded at Noise New York in January of 1988, have hit on local alternative radio. An EP (possibly an LP) will be produced by Kramer at Noise New York sometime this summer. Dean has a story about "Tugboat": "We had not finished that at all when we went into the recording studio. I wrote the lyrics in the ten minutes that I was waiting for Damon and Naomi to meet me. That's why they're so short. And, um, we hadn't worked out an ending to the song at all, so that was all largely improvised." Naomi said that when she designed the cover, "I was trying to give equal weight to both songs; I didn't want to imply an A side or a B side."

Naomi Yang was born in NYC in 1964 and is currently a grad student. Although she attended high school with Damon and Dean, she didn't begin performing out with them until the Autumn of '87. I asked her what made her decide to take up bass. "It was because Dean and Damon had played together in college, they had lost their bass player...I was really fed up with architecture school and I really liked the bass so I thought I'd try it and when I took it up I just really enjoyed it. I'd played all those kid instruments; the piano, the flute." Damon laughed. "Those are child's play!" Naomi continued: "Well, no one takes like, bass lessons as a five year old! Maybe, like, in some enlightened households! My first Rock & Roll memory was definitely The Beatles, because we all had to bring records into gym class in first grade; it was like, throwing balls around to music...and my good friend brought in The White Album and my other friend was saying, 'Which is your favorite song?', and one was like, "Rocky Racoon", and I was like, 'What is this?' and I was amazed at this, like, white record. I really liked the way it looked. I went home and lo and behold, my parents had it, next to the Pete Seeger records; I think I like, chewed on the poster and listened to it." When she was beginning to learn bass, Naomi listened to Public Image, New Order, Joy Division, and liked to play along to Jackson Five records. Another influence was Kendra Smith, who plays bass on The Dream Syndicate's first Lp. (It was Dean who introduced her to The Velvet Underground, and of course, J. Richman.)

Damon Krukowski was born in NYC in 1963; his mother was (and is) a jazz singer in the classic mode (Billie Holiday, Gershwin) and he grew up hearing a lot of great jazz: Miles Davis, Charlie Parker, Thelonious Monk, Ray Charles, Lester Young, MJQ and Duke Ellington. "Senior year in high school I took a few drum lessons with the percussion teacher at school, who was also with the NYC Opera, and he taught me the New Wave beat because I told him what kind of music I liked: Boomp-Pa-Toomp-Ba, Boomp-Pa-Toomp-Ba, which is indeed the basis of almost every NW song you ever listened to! [C.f. The Cars; "Start To Move" by Wire.] For me, it all started with The Clash. Topper Headon is the greatest R&R drummer ever. In college, Dean and another friend of ours named Mark formed Speedy and The Castanets. 1981. It was our bass player's idea. Corey Brennan produced our first demo tape, with borrowed equipment from WHRB. The band lasted two years, 'til Mark had a sudden conversion to Christianity and decided that R&R was the Devil's instrument. We played with a couple other bass players here and there, then we graduated in '85. Dean went away; Naomi and I stayed to go to grad school and we talked Dean into moving back last September. In fact, I had mucical training in piano; I also played guitar for at least a month. And because you can never be off-key on the drums. Harmony absolutely bewildered me. I never understood why any note wasn't OK at any moment. But then I had a theory for awhile that it wouldn't matter when you hit the drums, because time is infinitely divisible, as [the Greek philosopher] Zeno told us. It's all about time. And that's why Topper Headon is a great drummer. And so is Scott Krauss from the original Pere Ubu. I guess it's a fallacy in Rock and Roll. It seemed to me that there was no reason why you couldn't hit the drum at any time and it wouldn't be in time in some time. The net result was that I couldn't play "Police and Thieves" properly, and no one would listen to Speedy and The Castenets. In S&TC we also played our own songs, like "Alienation Across the Nation" (we were kind of political.) We used to open for dance cover bands at college dances, and no one would be there except our nearest and dearest friends and they would applaud after the better of The Clash covers that we did. The other bands would borrow our drums and amps, that was why they'd let us play! They'd give us $50 and we would have to stay there until three in the morning. We'd play "I'm So Bored With The USA", "Train In Vain", "Garageland". [Naomi mentions "Submission" by The Sex Pistols; Dean claims they also did "The Spider Man Theme".] "We played "Human Fly"--the Cramps do it--and "Leaving on a Jet Plane". But I played guitar on that!"

Dean Wareham was born 1963, in Wellington, New Zealand. His parents moved to Sydney, Australia in 1970 and to NYC in 1977. He claims he didn't experience very much culture shock, and that the Australian Top 40 was a good deal like its American counterpart. "My older brother gave me his Lou Reed and David Bowie records. My dad used to play a lot of Elvis Presley, like late, more baroque, as you say..."Suspicious Minds", I love that song. My dad is a management consultant. He moved to NYC to set up business over here. I was trying to put together a band in NY for like a year. After I graduated I went to Germany, and came back, 1986. We started playing over that summer in New York and I decided I had nothing better to do than to move back to Boston. Recently we've been practicing for two hours, three times a week." Dean says he hates to write lyrics, but when I asked him who wrote the words for "Tugboat", he admitted they were his. I asked him if the song was a reflection of his viewpoint. "Sometimes. Yeah. Like...after a beer. Although it was written in the morning. I used to really like political music, but I really don't have an aesthetic theory to justify the kinds of songs I write. I'm much more into playing the guitar. Some people say we sound like The Velvet Underground, but that's said about every second band that comes along." Damon laughs and says, "But it's true about us!" Dean continues: "David Greene [WMBR] said we sounded like The Feelies. And I feel they're the greatest. With the possible exception of Pere Ubu." The conversation shifts to The Velvet Underground, and specifically to the live 2 LP set '69.

Damon: That's the finest. **Dean**: What does that say, that that's the finest? It says that John Cale is nothing to the band! He said 'We never lived up to our promise', which is a suggestion that when he left, the whole band went downhill, which I think is...rubbish. The thing that is great about '69 is these pounding guitar rhythms, endlessly, repetitively simple. The lesson I have learned--maybe--from Lou Reed's guitar playing is that there are countless guitarists out there who are technical geniuses, who can do amazing things and play one string with both hands--but there's also an intense pleasure to be gotten out of a simple chord change from like, say, a G chord to a D chord, or a G to a C...if you do it right, anyway." **Damon**: My little brother, who knows a lot of musical theory, says that the hot new musical theory is that all there is to music is like a 1-5-1 chord progression, which is like saying that all there is, is The Velvet Underground, which is pretty amusing. Mo Tucker is a genius. Not her singing. **Dean**: She's the only one of them who's remained at all true to the spirit of what they were doing. The primitivism of it."

Towards the end of the interview, Damon makes a couple of interesting comments about music: "The trap drum kit comes from vaudeville, the drummer who used to sit in the orchestra pit. The drumkit was just a makeshift invention. Jazz made use of the marginal instruments of the classical orchestra. A lot of marching band instruments, essentially. And R&R has centered itself on marginal instruments out of jazz--guitar and bass, essentially. Dean notes that Pere Ubu felt confined by Rock and Roll instruments, and that on their later records they evolved away from them. He mentions there's a new Pere Ubu album, offers to tape it for me, and then Galaxie 500 bids me farewell--off to one of their thrice-weekly practice sessions. A week earlier I had asked them how long they planned to stay in Boston. Dean said, "We see Boston as Hamburg". Damon said, "Chet's was the Cavern Club". Naomi said "Until we get our degrees." Damon: "A year and a half." And then? Damon: "Move back to New York."

So be advised, and catch them while you can.

Poster, Summer 1988.
Neither we nor the venue were officially part of the New Music Seminar, but we managed to get a gig while it was going on and talked the bar into allowing pass holders in for free.

A tapebox with Damon's, Dean's, and Kramer's writing on it.
It looks like this reel began as our first session with Kramer (including the version of "Oblivious" given to *Chemical Imbalance*)—then reused during the *On Fire* sessions—it seems to have served as the *Blue Thunder* EP master at some point—and finally ended up with the *On Fire* outtakes that we later released on the Rykodisc box set.

I was at Kramer + Sheena's house in the morning + there was all this bustling around because each animal had its own specific very complicated breakfast that had to be made. So Kramer was making all this weird stuff in blenders and giving each animal its own food. Before he had even eaten.

I went outside with Sheena, + was a beautiful shining beach with a long row of palm trees swaying in the wind. Sheena started to speak spanish + a line of mermaids appeared on the beach with opalescent veils flowing all around. The mermaids wanted to speak to Sheena in private. So I sat very quietly in the corner reading Tintin books, while the mermaids put a shining veil over Sheena, and spoke with her very softly.

A dream I had about Kramer and Sheena, Spring 1988.
Sheena was the pen name for Shannon, Kramer's wife at the time, who did much of the Shimmy Disc artwork and later designed many t-shirts for us.

T-shirt design by Shannon Kramer.
Aztec calendar with stylized maize and psychedelic typography.

T-shirt design by Shannon Kramer.
This one featured a glow-in-the-dark green ink.
The image is from an infrared photo of us in the woods taken by Michael Macioce.

Fall 1988–1989

TOMMY JOHNSON
566-3339

	Monday	Tuesday	Wednesday	Thursday	Friday	Saturday	Sunday
September	29	30	31	1	2	3	4
	5 Labor Day	6	7	8	9	10	11
	12	13	14	15 **Orientation and Registration**	16 **Studio Lottery**	17	18
	19 **Classes Begin**	20	21	22 Green St.	23	24	25 FNX coop
October	26	27	28	29	30	1	2 FNX?
	3 BUNRATTY'S	4 CZECH	5	6	7	8	9
	10 Columbus Day	11	12	13	14 CHANNEL -FNX-	15	16 Green St.
	17	18	19	20	21 RAT	22	23
	24	25 CZECH	26	27	28	29 CBGB'S CANTEEN	30
November	31	1	2	3 Green St. - ½ JAP	4 **Module 1 Ends**	5	6
	7 **Module 2 Begins**	8	9	10 M.I.T.	11 A.R.T. Veteran's Day	12 HAMPSHIRE w/ B.A.L.L.	13
	14	15 CZECH	16	17	18 MAXWELL's w/ P. Galore	19	20
	21	22	23	24 **Thanksgiving Recess**	25	26	27
December	28	29	30	1 AXIS Crime + The City	2	3	4
	5	6 CZECH	7	8	9	10	11
	12	13 CBGB'S SONIC YOUTH B.A.L.L.	14	15	16 Pixies at RAT	17	18
	19 **Winter Recess Begins**	20	21	22	23	24	25 Christmas Day
January	26 University Holiday	27	28	29	30 Record CANTEEN	31	1 New Year's Day
	2 **Winter Recess Ends** University Holiday	3	4	5	6 **Classes End**	7	8
	9 **Exam Period Begins**	10	11	12	13	14	15
	16 Martin Luther King, Jr. Day	17 N's FINAL REVIEW Term Paper	18	19	20 **Exam Period Ends** Big Dipper PARADISO	21 → $500	22
	23 **Midyear Break Begins**	24	25	26	27 **Midyear Break Ends**	28	29

Graduate School of Design calendar, Fall 1988–Spring 1989.
By the spring I had left school to go on tour. I notice at that point the handwriting changes, it is Damon's, not mine, and we are using the calendar only to keep track of gigs.

Spring 1988–1989

	Monday	Tuesday	Wednesday	Thursday	Friday	Saturday	Sunday
February	**30** **Studio Lottery**	**31** **Classes Begin** **Registration**	**1**	**2**	**3**	**4** T.T.'s w/ Volcano Suns	**5** → $150
	6	**7**	**8** NOISE	**9** →	**10**	**11**	**12**
	13	**14**	**15**	**16**	**17**	**18** Middlebury →	**19** $750 (-$100)
	20 Presidents' Day	**21**	**22**	**23**	**24**	**25** RAT w/ BALL	**26** → $200
March	**27**	**28**	**1**	**2**	**3**	**4** AMHERST $350	**5**
	6	**7**	**8**	**9**	**10**	**11**	**12**
	13	**14**	**15**	**16**	**17** **Module 3 Ends**	**18** $250 Green St. Yo La Tengo	**19**
	20 **Module 4 Begins**	**21**	**22**	**23**	**24** CAR PARTY RENT NY HERTZ [illegible]	**25**	**26**
April	**27** **Spring Recess Begins**	**28**	**29** CHICAGO w/ [illegible]	**30**	**31** ST. LOUIS **Spring Recess Ends**	**1** Cincinnati	**2**
	3	**4**	**5**	**6** D.C. w/ [illegible]	**7**	**8** MAXWELL'S w/ [illegible]	**9**
	10	**11**	**12**	**13**	**14** Green Street	**15**	**16**
	17	**18**	**19**	**20**	**21** Commonwealth	**22**	**23**
	24	**25**	**26**	**27**	**28** Pyramid	**29** RAT	**30**
May	**1**	**2**	**3**	**4** Wellesley $400	**5**	**6**	**7**
	8	**9**	**10**	**11**	**12** T.T.'s **Classes End**	**13** CB'S 10:30–11:30	**14**
	15 **Exam Period Begins**	**16**	**17**	**18**	**19**	**20** Channel 11:00	**21**
	22	**23** PYRAMID	**24**	**25**	**26** **Exam Period Ends**	**27**	**28**
June	**29** Memorial Day	**30**	**31**	**1**	**2** Living Room w/ [illegible]	**3**	**4**
	5	**6**	**7**	**8** WBCN party **Commencement**	**9**	**10**	**11**
	12	**13**	**14**	**15**	**16**	**17**	**18**
	19	**20**	**21** Mid-Somerville [illegible]	**22**	**23**	**24**	**25**

following page **Poster for US tour, Spring 1989.**

GALAXIE 500
tourbillion
1989
AURORA RECORDS

DEAN WAREHAM: I hadn't taken a lot of lessons, so that limited what I could do anyway. But I liked players like Glenn Mercer of the Feelies—not a flamboyant player, but his playing is direct and melodic and he had a great tone. Or Jonathan Richman; we saw him stop a song in the middle of his guitar solo one night because he said he had wandered too far from the melody.

DAMON KRUKOWSKI: I think my favorite aspect of Dean's guitar playing was his tone—like on "When Will You Come Home," it's not about licks so much as making that particular amp sound that particular way. We each had so little to work with at first, both in terms of chops and equipment; I think it forced us all to do the most with the least, which is maybe what we were best at as a band.

DAVE RICK: Dean's early, smallish, high voice and subtle accent and laconic guitar were seated by Damon's spacious sound—long cymbal splashes, bottom heads on his sparkly Gretsch kit—and Naomi's unique, wide toned high on the neck melodies made a big, wide, slowly moving cloud.

FRANCIS DIMENNO: Very often, Dean basically sang like he didn't give a shit. Damon was a very versatile drummer, but not showy or flashy. And Naomi's bass playing was solid and unobtrusive. The band struck me as highly intelligent in a fairly uncommon way.

SIMON RAYMONDE: When you first get a band together, the influences of your record collections will be usually evident all over your first recordings, yet Galaxie 500 also managed to sound like no one else. For those of us who loved the Modern Lovers, Velvet Underground, Neil Young and etc., we found a new band with a new voice that filled the void those bands left.

KRAMER: On the first day of recording, I'll tell you what I thought. I thought Dean was just adequate as a guitar player; I wondered if he could play more than two or three chords. Damon? I thought, this takes guts to play almost nothing. But when I heard Naomi, my heart started to pound in my chest. What she did with the bass made my heart pound.

DAMON KRUKOWSKI: The bass was the physical center of the band, from my point of view behind the drums. Guitar on top; drums at bottom; bass in the middle. It all hung off the bass. I used to keep the bass so loud in my monitor; it was almost all I heard when we played live.

NAOMI YANG: I always thought of the bass lines as alternative melodies, or counter-melodies. I picked up the bass without knowing how to play it, and took a few lessons where the teacher was showing me the way to play bass "properly," but that just seemed totally boring to me. I had all these melodies going around my head, and I just decided to play bass that way. It just seemed more natural to me, and it seemed to add more to the song than what I was "supposed" to play on the bass. I usually played only on the top two strings of my bass, as that mirrored my vocal range.

DEAN WAREHAM: Like me, Naomi hadn't been playing that long. But she had really good taste, which is as important as anything, and quickly developed a melodic style and her own sound too. Those Gibson basses were an oddity (Peter Hook played one too).

CHRIS XEFOS: Naomi's playing really blew me away (being a bass player myself), though really they all brought unique elements to the table: Damon's jazzy yet strong approach to the drum kit, and Dean's minimalist but strong guitar style—and how they all brought it together with Dean's vocals and crazy lyrics.

SIMON RAYMONDE: It's unique for a trio to be able to all be individuals inside the group sound without there seeming to be one star performer. Girl bass players weren't exactly common, and I really liked her simple naive approach. It was perfect and was just cool. Dean played a Gibson, which we all did, so he was cool; he had great shirts and that Velvets-y delivery with smart lyrics, so it was a winning combination. Damon wasn't just a straight rock or pop drummer, he was expressive, and these parts made the band so special.

NAOMI YANG: Maybe it is because we have been playing together for so long, but to me Damon's playing just seems effortless—the way a drummer should sound. It is very musical and not predictable—restrained when it has to be and dramatic when it has to be. I always loved watching Damon play—his mother was a dancer and Damon is a great dancer too—he is very graceful.

DEAN WAREHAM: I love Damon's playing. If you listen to "Flowers," which is one of our earlier songs, the way he dances around the snare is beautiful, it's a surprise each time he hits it. I don't think of him as "kick ass" (any more than I think of Ringo Starr that way), but he picked his moments to do that, and that's what made them dramatic. I've played with some great drummers who have trouble getting the Galaxie 500 songs.

PHIL McMULLEN (*writer*): I produced a rather hyperbole-drenched piece for the *Ptolemaic Terrascope* which spoke of their sound as akin to "being murdered by butterflies, enveloped in a million fragments of near silence which suffocate you with accumulated noise." I'm not sure I even have the excuse of having been hallucinating when I wrote that.

MARTIN ASTON: Together, and apart, they had simplicity, drama, and all that interlocking-puzzle stuff particular to trios. Damon didn't play traditionally, but splashed around the kit. Meshed with Naomi's rudimentary innocence, and then Dean's spangling feedbacking sound. How else to put it? If I could play guitar, that's how I would have played.

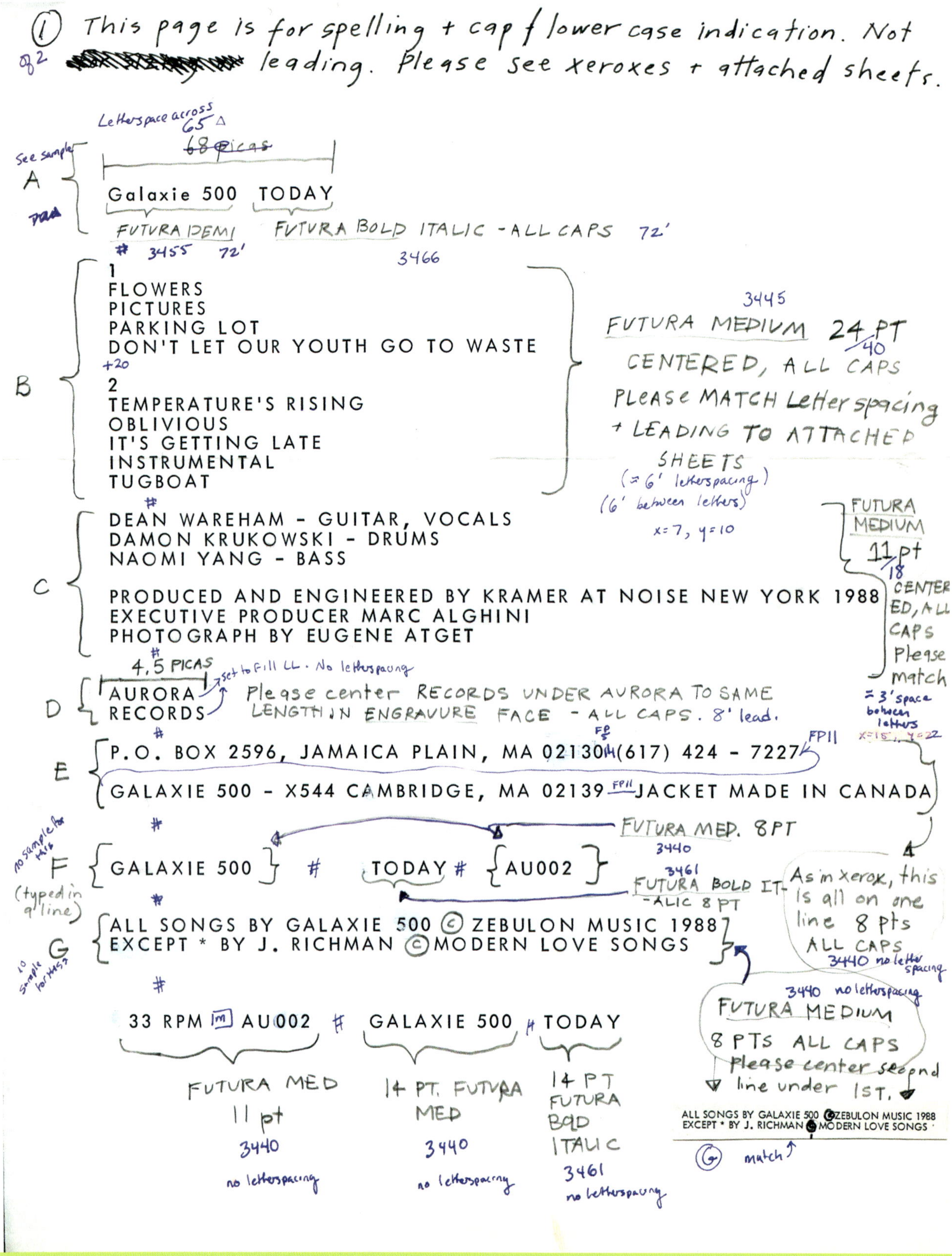

① This page is for spelling + cap / lower case indication. Not leading. Please see xeroxes + attached sheets.

A — Letterspace across 65 (~~68 picas~~) — see sample

Galaxie 500 TODAY

FUTURA DEMI # 3455 72' / FUTURA BOLD ITALIC - ALL CAPS 72' 3466

B — FUTURA MEDIUM 24 PT / 40 (3445), CENTERED, ALL CAPS. PLEASE MATCH Letterspacing + LEADING TO ATTACHED SHEETS (= 6' letterspacing) (6' between letters) x=7, y=10

1
FLOWERS
PICTURES
PARKING LOT
DON'T LET OUR YOUTH GO TO WASTE

2
TEMPERATURE'S RISING
OBLIVIOUS
IT'S GETTING LATE
INSTRUMENTAL
TUGBOAT

C — FUTURA MEDIUM 11 pt / 18, CENTERED, ALL CAPS. Please match = 3' space between letters

DEAN WAREHAM - GUITAR, VOCALS
DAMON KRUKOWSKI - DRUMS
NAOMI YANG - BASS

PRODUCED AND ENGINEERED BY KRAMER AT NOISE NEW YORK 1988
EXECUTIVE PRODUCER MARC ALGHINI
PHOTOGRAPH BY EUGENE ATGET

D — 4.5 PICAS — set to fill LL. No letterspacing

AURORA
RECORDS

Please center RECORDS UNDER AURORA TO SAME LENGTH IN ENGRAVURE FACE - ALL CAPS. 8' lead.

E

P.O. BOX 2596, JAMAICA PLAIN, MA 02130 (617) 424 - 7227
GALAXIE 500 - X544 CAMBRIDGE, MA 02139 JACKET MADE IN CANADA

F (typed in a line) — no sample for this

GALAXIE 500 # TODAY # AU002

FUTURA MED. 8 PT 3440 / FUTURA BOLD ITALIC 8 PT 3461

G — no sample for this

ALL SONGS BY GALAXIE 500 © ZEBULON MUSIC 1988
EXCEPT * BY J. RICHMAN © MODERN LOVE SONGS

As in xerox, this is all on one line 8 pts ALL CAPS 3440 no letter spacing

FUTURA MEDIUM 8 PTS ALL CAPS 3440 no letterspacing. Please center second line under 1st.

ALL SONGS BY GALAXIE 500 © ZEBULON MUSIC 1988
EXCEPT * BY J. RICHMAN © MODERN LOVE SONGS

Ⓖ match

33 RPM AU002 # GALAXIE 500 # TODAY

FUTURA MED 11 pt 3440 no letterspacing / 14 PT. FUTURA MED 3440 no letterspacing / 14 PT FUTURA BOLD ITALIC 3461 no letterspacing

My typesetting instructions for the *Today* LP.
Thank God for Apple computers!

Today album cover, 1988.

TODAY

IS it a band or a new astrological configuration? Music is the backbeat of the stars; and for once Amerrican space travel pays off.

From the furthest reaches of space, that is, Kramer's Noise NY studio, float a few celestial riffs and sppooky knocks. The lyrics were picked up by antenna. And only Kramer knows what else snuck in while the chanells were open.

On Saturn they're only just picking up our 1967 broadcasts. And the bartender says: these guys have a sound.

The sound is today. A few light years away, but it's still now. Flying out of the mystery and back in your life. By laser beamm.

Mickey Zebulon

A draft of the liner notes for the European release of *Today* on CD.
Mickey Zebulon was a collective pseudonym.

Promo photo, 1988.
I took this myself in Dean's old apartment in Jamaica Plain, Boston. I placed Dean and Damon in the frame, then sat between them and pressed the bulb release. I rented a motor for the day so the camera would advance itself. Outtakes and contact sheet overleaf.

Who is Galaxie 500?

Drummer Damon Krukowski, born in New York City.
Guitarist/Vocalist Dean Wareham, born in New Zealand.
Bassist Naomi Yang, born in New York City.

Galaxie 500 formed in New York City in the summer of 1987 and moved to Boston three months later. Since arriving on the local scene they have been recognized as Boston's most happening new band, immediately charting on the hippest college radio stations with their tapes -- "Walking Song", "Oblivious", and "Tugboat". The band was quickly signed to fledgling local label Aurora Records, which released the single "Tugboat"/"King of Spain".

The 9-song LP you have in your hands was recorded at Noise New York in July 1988 (with the exception of "Tugboat", recorded at Noise earlier in the year), and was produced by Kramer (Bongwater, B.A.L.L., Shockabilly, Shimmy-Disc, etc.). The LP features eight new Galaxie 500 compositions and one cover version, a re-working of Jonathan Richman's "Don't Let Our Youth Go to Waste," (originally a 50-second acappella song).

The original (radio-tape only) recording of "Oblivious" will be available on a 7" single enclosed in the next issue of Chemical Imbalance magazine, along with cuts by Half Japanese and Daniel Johnston.

AURORA RECORDS, P.O. BOX 2596, Jamaica Plain, MA 02130

Celebrating the release of the album

TODAY

by

GALAXIE 500

Aurora Records invites you to a party

FRIDAY OCTOBER 21 at THE RAT

8:00 to 9:30 food will be provided
Music from 9:30 and on with
SALEM 66, the CAVEDOGS,
and BITCH MAGNET

GALAXIE 500 will play a set at 10:15
This invitation admits you and a guest

Aurora Records 424-7227

◀ Aurora Records press release, 1988.

▲ Invitation to record release party, Fall 1988.

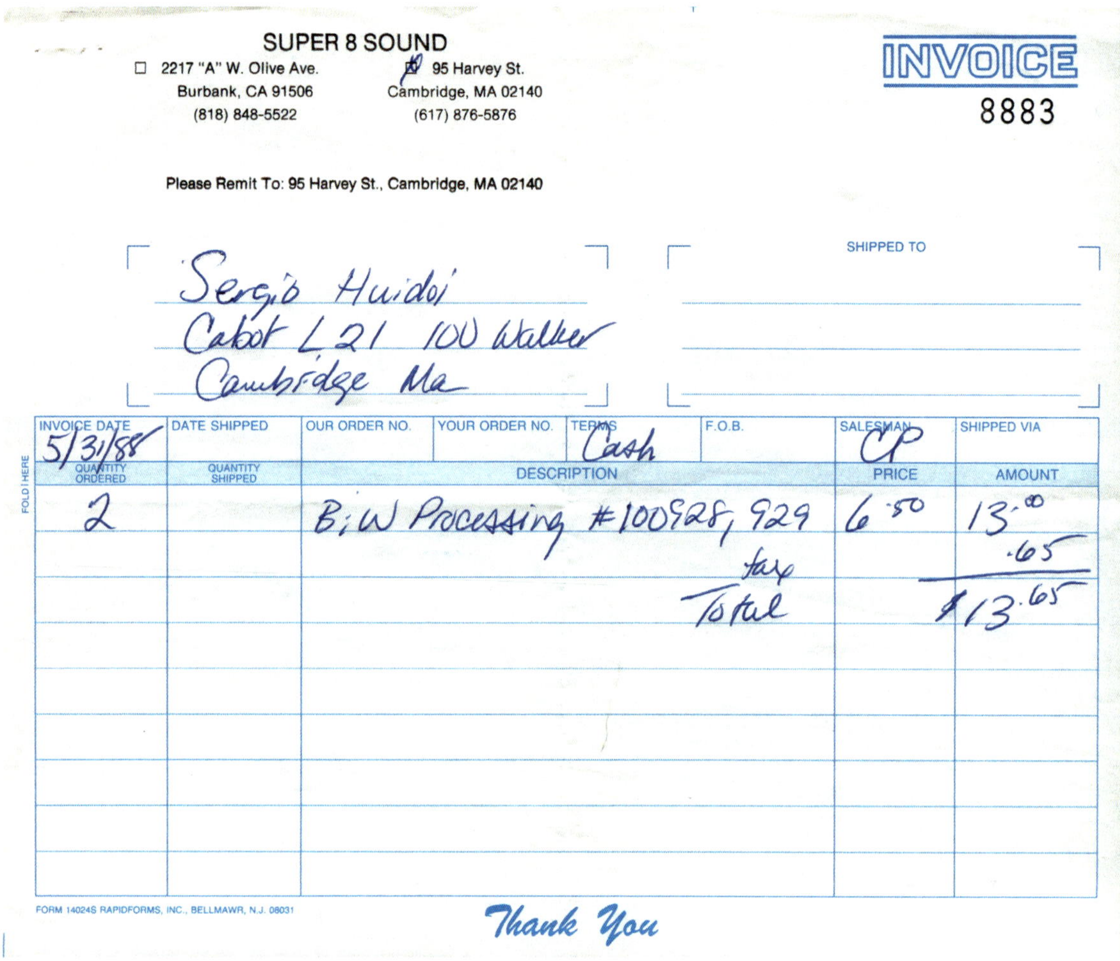

SUPER 8 SOUND

☐ 2217 "A" W. Olive Ave. Burbank, CA 91506 (818) 848-5522

☒ 95 Harvey St. Cambridge, MA 02140 (617) 876-5876

INVOICE

8883

Please Remit To: 95 Harvey St., Cambridge, MA 02140

Sergio Huidor
Cabot L21 100 Walker
Cambridge Ma

SHIPPED TO

INVOICE DATE	DATE SHIPPED	OUR ORDER NO.	YOUR ORDER NO.	TERMS	F.O.B.	SALESMAN	SHIPPED VIA
5/31/88				Cash		CP	

QUANTITY ORDERED	QUANTITY SHIPPED	DESCRIPTION	PRICE	AMOUNT
2		B/W Processing #100928, 929	6.50	13.00
		tax		.65
		Total		$13.65

FOLD HERE

FORM 14024S RAPIDFORMS, INC., BELLMAWR, N.J. 08031

Thank You

"Tugboat" video receipts, 1988.

Sergio Huidor and I were friends from the art department at Harvard. He borrowed a school camera and shot Super 8, transferred it to VHS tape, and then edited it using two VCR machines. Total cost…under $100.

ECLIPSE VIDEO SERVICES, INC.
95 HARVEY STREET
CAMBRIDGE, MA 02140
(617) 491-1714

NO 2359

CUST. ORDER NO.	PHONE	DATE 6-6-88

SOLD TO Damon Krkowski
ADDRESS 888 Mass Ave., Camb.

☐ CASH ☐ CR. CD. ☐ MDSE. RET'D. SOLD BY
☐ C.O.D. ☐ ON ACCT. ☐ PAID OUT

QTY.	DESCRIPTION	UNIT PRICE	AMOUNT
	transfer to Tape & Rush		51 25
1	Maxell T-120 HGX		7 00
	Paid Cash		
			58 25
RECEIVED BY	Total 61.16	TAX	2 91
		TOTAL	61 16

THIS SLIP MUST ACCOMPANY ANY RETURNS OR CLAIMS ORIGINAL

Thank You

On tour in the US, with Dave Rick as driver/roadie and voice of experience, Spring 1989.

Phone

The Paradise, Boston, 1989.

On Fire album cover, 1989.

NAOMI YANG: We would not have been the same band without Kramer—his production, his arrangements and his attitude to recording formed us as young musicians. He had a very strong aesthetic, and for the most part we welcomed his collaboration. I think later, as we became more experienced musicians, we began to have more of our own ideas about where to take the music, but we learned so much from him.

DEAN WAREHAM: It's hard to know what we would have sounded like without him. It's kind of amazing how great he made us sound on that first LP, and within just a few days. If producing is a matter of making the right decisions, and making them quickly, then that's certainly what he did. He didn't play the instruments for us (except piano, keys, or the occasional backing vocal), but he situated us in a particular sonic space and made our small band sound big.

MARTIN ASTON: Just for the sonic mood, he was their Martin Hannett. He did it quickly—because he was such a cheapskate, probably, or got bored easily, but also he recognized that their sound was not for honing and doing 47 takes. Dean's vocal would have suffered if he'd been corseted and had to repeat himself over and over

DAMON KRUKOWSKI: Quick doesn't do Kramer's system justice. "Next!" No second takes. We had to come in very prepared. Any mistake you made, you knew it was going to end up on the record. Kramer loves mistakes.

TERRY TOLKIN (*record buyer, Caroline; later A&R, Rough Trade US*): Kramer had a lot to do with the muted, ethereal vibe. He really got this right on *Today* and *On Fire*. Kramer is the reverb king. It covers up mistakes and moves you onto the next passage. It's a technique that he's employed his whole career with great success.

NAOMI YANG: Working with Kramer was quick—but also so slow! When he was working we had to do everything fast, in one or two takes. He had very limited patience; I think because he is such a facile musician himself, he just couldn't imagine making simple mistakes, or not singing perfectly in key. But when he got distracted, by his business or personal life, he would disappear for hours—the three of us would just be sitting in the studio saying to each other, I wonder when he is coming back. Many people didn't work with him because they couldn't put up with that. But we were always so pleased with what he did with the music in the end, that we did.

SIMON RAYMONDE: I know Dean was always complimentary about what he brought to the band; I sometimes think producers get too much credit.

DEAN WAREHAM: He just really did not see the point in recording a song twelve different times, or agonizing for hours over a guitar solo. We would do one take (or occasionally two) of the basics: bass, drums and guitar. Then I would record my vocal, and add a second guitar (and too bad if I played a bad note because he would say that it added flavor). And Damon would add percussion parts. And then Kramer might add his own thing, like a piano or fake-string arrangement. Then he would mix each song in an hour or less.

MICHAEL MACIOCE (*Photographer*): The first time we did a photo shoot, we went to a park in Queens. I had them walk into the trees; I was thinking of an ELP record, Trilogy. I used color infrared film for a '60s psychedelic feel. After the film came back we met up at Noise New York on Walker Street. We were in the studio when I showed them the pictures. They were so polite, very respectful of us, being a bit older, and I think they were not crazy about the shots.

Kramer said, "Look at them! You look like Ten Years After!" And Galaxie stared back blankly. "Ten Years After!" Kramer said again. I looked from face to face. "Ten Years After? Woodstock?" That may have been the first time I realized I was now older than the bands I photographed. They didn't use the picture for an album, but Kramer made a shirt from it.

BYRON COLEY: For all his boob stonerism, Mark [Kramer's rarely-heard first name] came up with some excellent studio sound, and was definitely a big part of the recorded legacy of the band.

DAMON KRUKOWSKI: Kramer invented the sound of the band. I mean, we already had the songs—we came in and played them first take; there was no composing in the studio. But Kramer taught us about overdubs, and through that he taught us about arranging—he showed us how to complicate what we were doing. And in a lot of ways, I think we learned from our own records how to be Galaxie 500. We couldn't have written the songs for *On Fire* without learning to play the way Kramer had made us sound on *Today*.

Photos taken at the site of the 1964 World's Fair in Queens, NY, 1989.
These are by Michael Macioce, Shimmy Disc house photographer and Kramer's oldest friend. He often used infrared film, both color and black-and-white, to dramatic effect—everything glowed, and the colors were all unexpected.

Photos by Michael Macioce, 1989.

KRAMER
247 West Broadway
NEW YORK, NEW YORK 10013
PM
25 JUL
1989
Bread Wagon 1880s
25 USA
YOUR
APT
FOR
BETTER
Damon Krukowski
888 Mass. Ave
#517
Cambridge, MA. 02139

Producers Notes

JAF Box 1187 • New York, NY • 10116
(212) 334-4134

THEN THERE WAS THE GREAT CHICAGO FIRE. I WAS THERE. THE STORIES OF HOW THE FIRE BEGAN WERE WILDLY CONTRADICTORY, BUT I WAS THERE. SOME PEOPLE SAY THE FIRE WAS STARTED BY A STAMPEDE OF COWS. SOME SAY IT WAS JUST ONE COW. SOME TRIED TO BLAME IT ALL ON SOMEONE THEY DIDN'T LIKE. ONE FELLA TRIED TO BLAME IT ON HIS OWN BROTHER, JUST BECAUSE HIS BROTHER HAD STOLEN AWAY HIS GIRLFRIEND AND MARRIED HER. THE WEDDING TOOK PLACE IN LAS VEGAS. IT WAS A MODEST AFFAIR OF ABOUT 150 GUESTS, NON-DENOMINATIONAL (WHICH REALLY PISSED OFF THE PARENTS OF THE BRIDE, BUT HELL, YOU CAN'T PLEASE EVERYBODY). DURING THE CEREMONY, SOME ROTTEN LITTLE PUNKS YELLED "FIRE! FIRE!" AND THE WHOLE PLACE CLEARED OUT IN NO TIME. THE MAID OF HONOR EVEN BROKE HER ANKLE IN 2 PLACES AFTER BEING SHOVED DOWN THE ALTER BY THE ALWAYS OVERLY ZEALOUS JUSTICE OF THE PEACE. WELL, THE ANKLE WAS PRETTY BAD AND THE MAID OF HONOR HAD TO BE SHOT, AND EXACTLY ONE WEEK LATER THE ENTIRE BLOCK BURNED TO THE GROUND. EVEN THE BRICKS BURNED. BUT AT LEAST NOBODY TRIED TO BLAME IT ON A COW. AND THE WEDDING WENT AHEAD AS PLANNED. AND SOME PEOPLE ACTUALLY BELIEVE THAT NERO FIDDLED AS ROME BURNED, AND THAT HE REALLY DID LOOK LIKE A BADLY AGING PETER LORRE. ON SUNDAY NIGHTS WE'D ALL GATHER 'ROUND THE TELEVISION SET TO WATCH THE DISNEY SHOW, AND I WOULD ALWAYS FALL ASLEEP FROM BOREDOM. BUT I HAD A BIG OL' SIAMESE CAT NAMED BUTCH WHO'D ALWAYS LOVED TO PLAY WITH MY FACE WITHIN MOMENTS AFTER MY HEAD HIT THE PILLOW. SO I'D AWAKE STARTLED, SOMETIMES CRYING, SOMETIMES COVERED WITH BLOOD AND CRYING, STARING INTO THE IDIOT BOX. SOMETIMES I'D SEE WALT HIMSELF, SOMETIMES MICKEY OR GOOFY. BUT SOMETIMES I'D SEE A THOUSAND BRIGHT BLUE CARIBOU RACING A DUST STORM TO THE FINISH LINE, NECK AND NECK ALL THE WAY LIKE NATURE'S OWN INDY 500 ! FLESH AND BLOOD AGAINST THE ELEMENTS! AND I REMEMBER WONDERING TO MYSELF..."WHY ARE THEY RACING?" THEN ONE FINE DAY I UNDERSTOOD WHY THE RACE TOOK PLACE. IT WAS BECAUSE THE HAIRS ON THOSE CARIBOU NECKS WERE BEING TICKLED BY THE INSTINCTUAL KNOWLEDGE OF A FIRE RAGING NOT TOO FAR AWAY, AND MOST CERTAINLY HEADED THIS WAY. HUMANS OFTEN GET THE SAME FEELING...LIKE AN ODDLY WARM BREEZE MALEVOLENTLY FUELED BY THE MADDENING FLAMES BEHIND IT. COME RIDE THE FIERY BREEZE OF GALAXIE 500!

Kramer, NYC
July 1989

Liner notes for *On Fire*, 1989.
I loved the old jazz album covers from Blue Note, and they always had liner notes by the producer on the back, so we asked Kramer to write something.

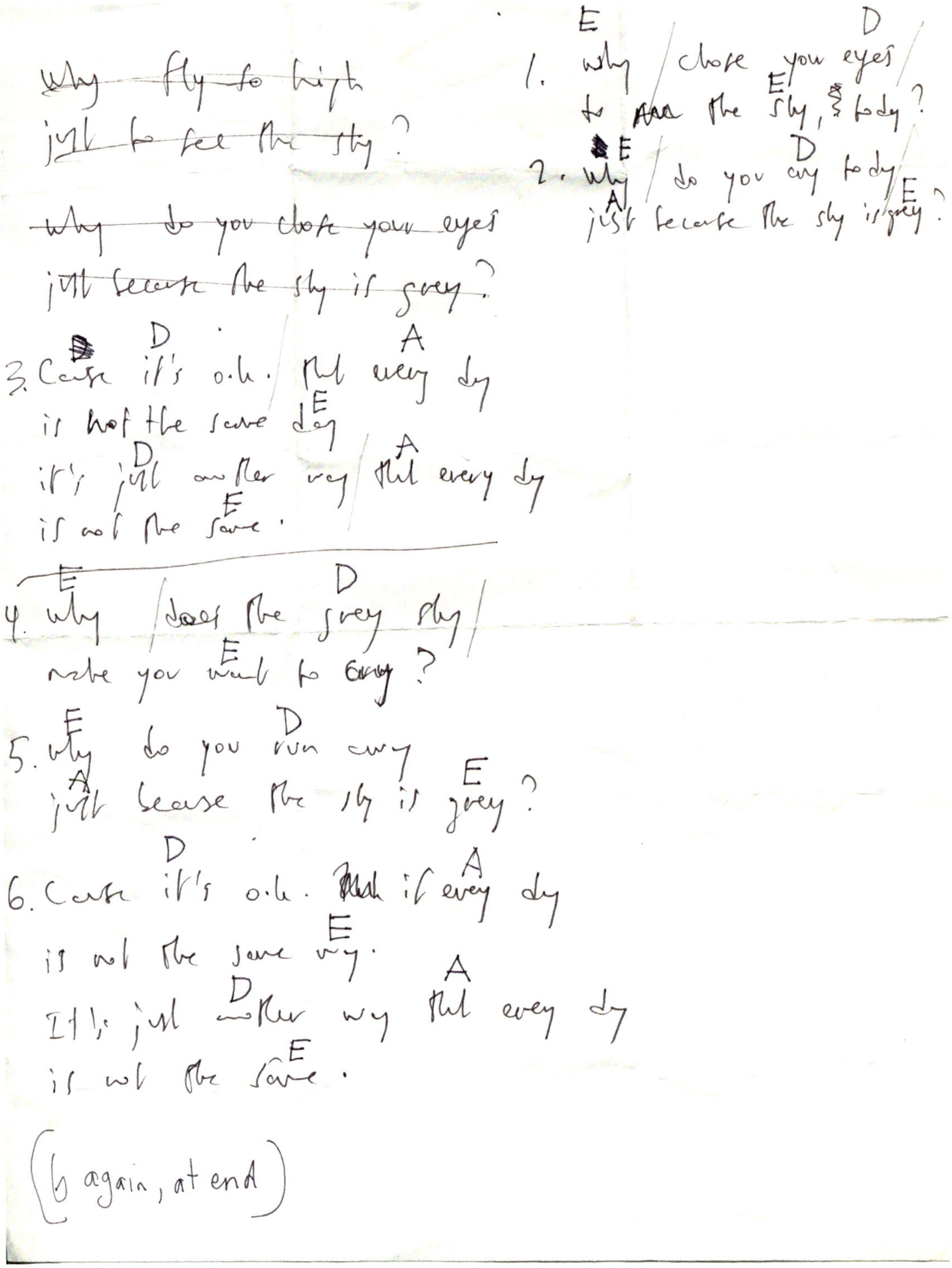

~~Why fly so high~~
~~just to see the sky?~~

~~why do you close your eyes~~
~~just because the sky is grey?~~

D A
3. Cause it's o.k. that every day
E
is not the same day
D A
it's just another way that every day
E
is not the same.

E D
4. why does the grey sky
E
make you want to cry?

E D
5. why do you run away
A E
just because the sky is grey?

D A
6. Cause it's o.k. that if every day
E
is not the same way.
D A
It's just another way that every day
E
is not the same.

(6 again, at end)

E D
1. why close your eyes
E
to see the sky, today?
E D
2. why do you cry today
A E
just because the sky is grey?

Lyric/chord sheet for "Another Day."

At Noise New York, recording *On Fire*, 1989.

Dean in the studio recording *On Fire*.

Damon in the studio recording *On Fire*.

Kramer recording *On Fire*.

In the studio recording *On Fire*.

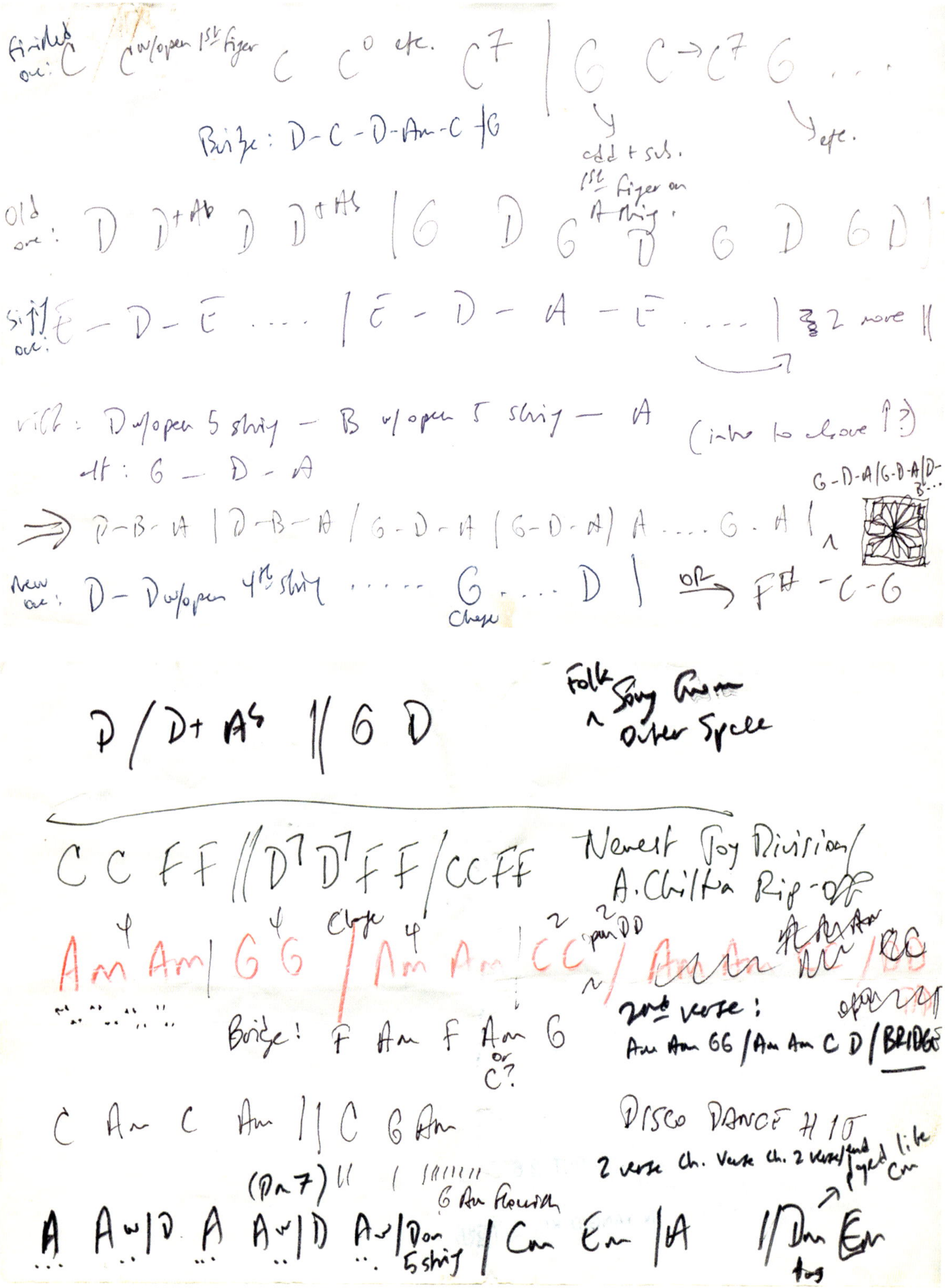

Damon's riff sheets.

The kind of notes Damon would bring into rehearsal. I like the working titles such as: "Newest Joy Division / A. Chilton Rip-off," or "Folk Song from Outer Space." The first riff, at the top of the upper page, eventually became "Blue Thunder."

DAMON KRUKOWSKI: The worst memory for me is probably also my first bad memory of the band: when we had a fight about songwriting credits just after finishing the first album. In fact, Naomi and I quit the band right then. *Today* wasn't even out yet. I mean, what was there to fight over? Naomi was preparing the album art when Dean said he wanted to divide up credits for the songs. That's certainly not weird in the context of the music business. But you know, up to that point I think neither Naomi or I had ever thought about the music as anything other than something we just did together—it wasn't about business, property, yours-and-mine. It was different from all that—which was exactly why we were doing it!

What followed was a farce. We said, well how are you going to decide whose songs are whose? And it turned out he didn't mean that any weren't his, just that some weren't ours! He said anything he had brought the guitar chords in for, was his. And we said ok, well then anything we brought the guitar chords in for, was ours. And he said but he wrote the lyrics for those, so they were his too. And we said, ok, so those will say music by us, lyrics by you. And now that's settled, we quit.

I guess what happened next is what allowed the band to continue. But it also set the pattern for everything that was wrong with it. We drew up a list of whose music was whose according to the cockamamie rules we'd worked out, and "Tugboat" ended up as ours, because I had brought in the guitar chords for that. And then Dean said he'd changed his mind. He wanted to go back to where we'd started—we'd share everything after all. And would we consider at least playing some shows when the album came out, since we'd all worked so hard on it?

So we did, and we ended up writing and rehearsing and playing just like before, which is how and why we kept going. But I could never know for sure whether we were a band again because Dean had decided that the original spirit we started with was a good thing, or because I happened to have brought in the chords—both of them!—for our first single. I think I convinced myself over and over that we were back where we'd started, only to find out again and again that we weren't. Or maybe it's more accurate to say that we'd never really been there in the first place.

DEAN WAREHAM: It felt that way to me [getting ganged up on]. I thought that when we came to decide which songs would go on the first album, that they had decided together already, and that was that. I'm sure that's pretty hard to avoid if you're a couple, and they maybe didn't even realize it was going on, but it was problematic in a three piece band.

Sergio Huidor filming the "When Will You Come Home" video in our practice space, Boston, 1989.

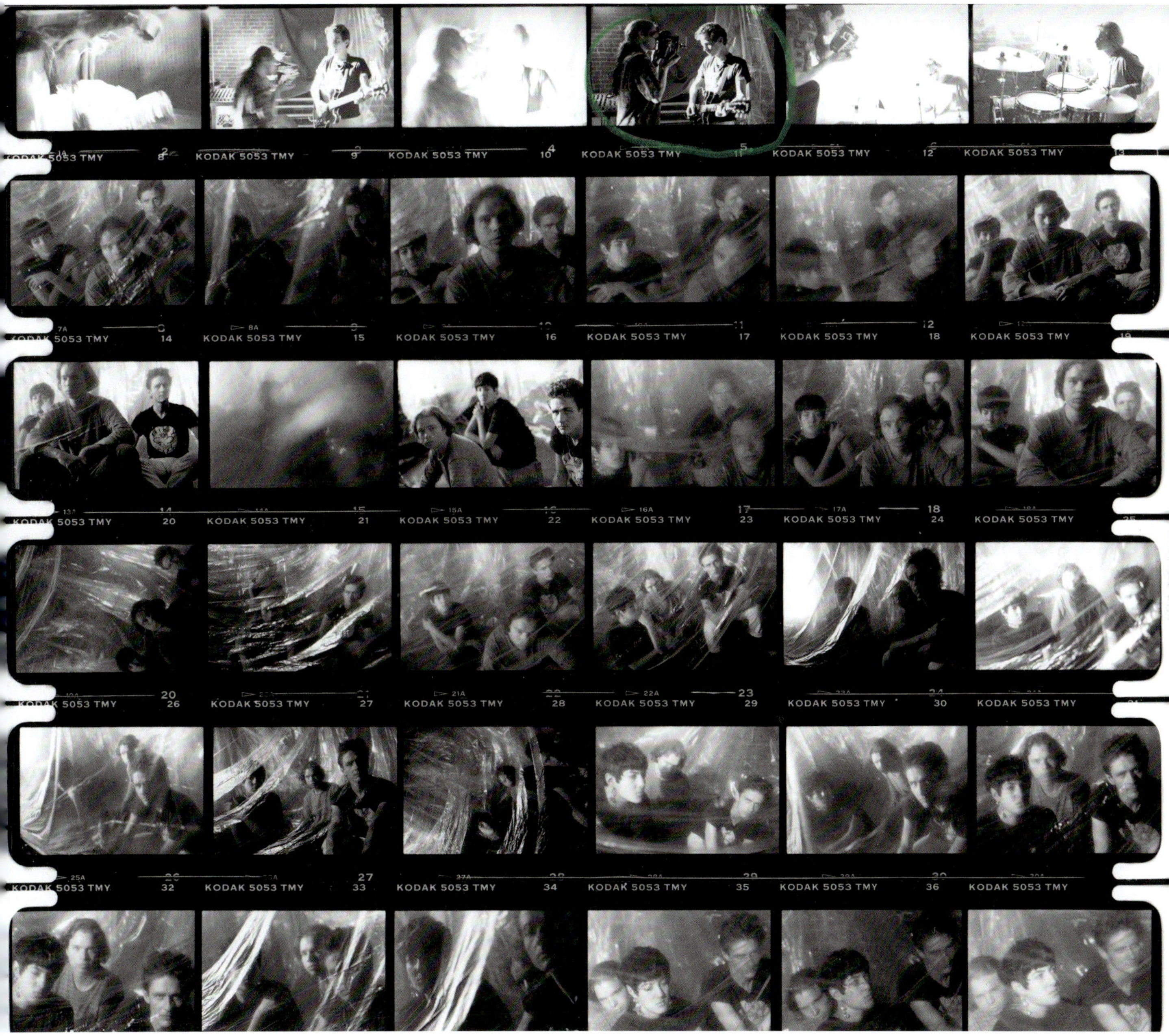
KODAK 5053 TMY KODAK 5053 TMY KODAK 5053 TMY KODAK 5053 TMY KODAK 5053 TMY KODAK 5053 TMY
KODAK 5053 TMY KODAK 5053 TMY KODAK 5053 TMY KODAK 5053 TMY KODAK 5053 TMY KODAK 5053 TMY
KODAK 5053 TMY KODAK 5053 TMY KODAK 5053 TMY KODAK 5053 TMY KODAK 5053 TMY KODAK 5053 TMY
KODAK 5053 TMY KODAK 5053 TMY KODAK 5053 TMY KODAK 5053 TMY KODAK 5053 TMY KODAK 5053 TMY
KODAK 5053 TMY KODAK 5053 TMY KODAK 5053 TMY KODAK 5053 TMY KODAK 5053 TMY KODAK 5053 TMY

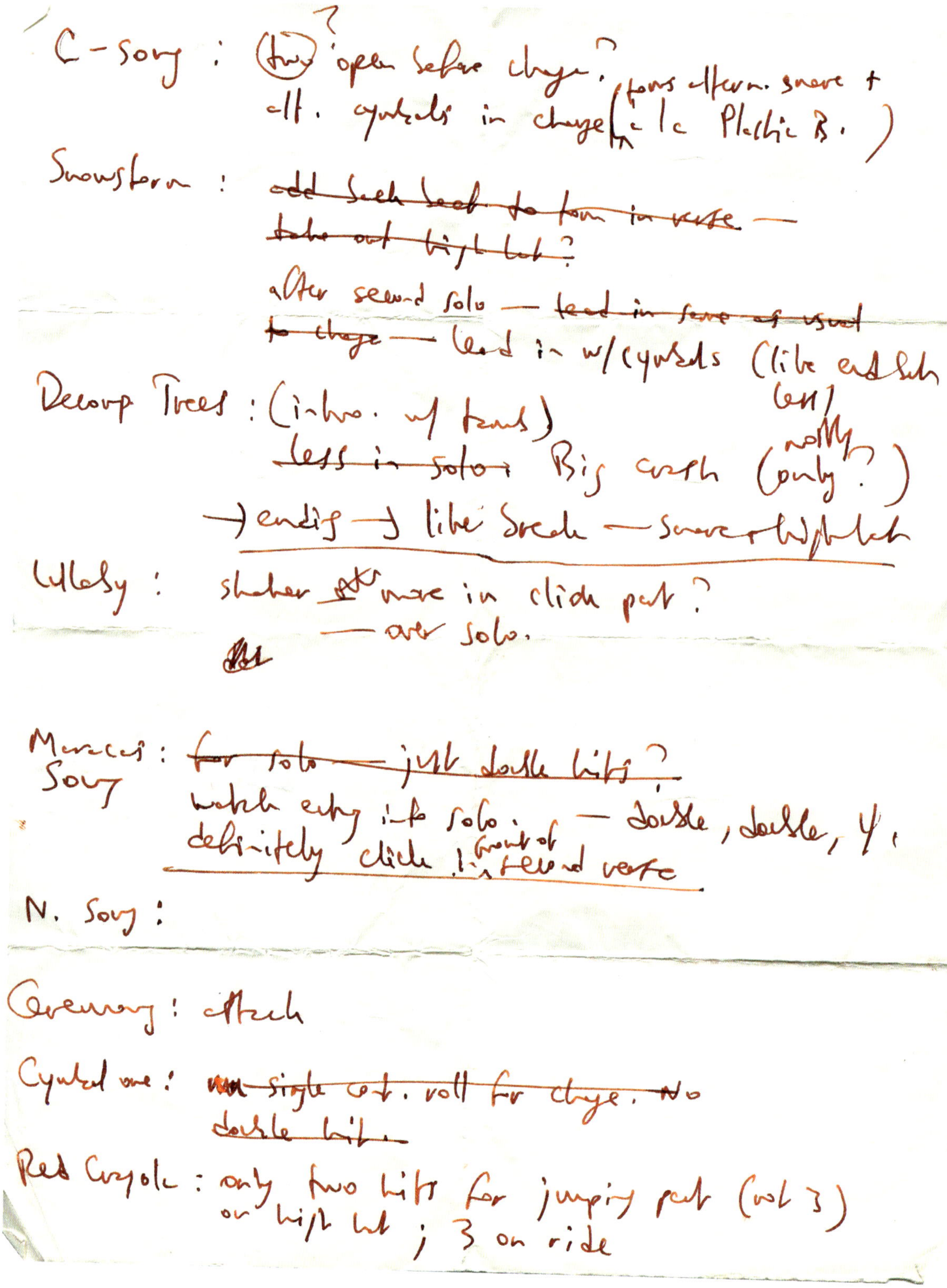

C-Song: (two)? open before change? (toms alternate snare + alt. cymbals in change (à la Plastic B.)

Snowstorm: ~~add such beat to tom in verse~~ — ~~take out high hat?~~
after second solo — ~~lead in same as usual to change~~ — lead in w/ cymbals (like end sub beat)

Decomp Trees: (intro. w/ toms)
~~less in solo~~ Big crash (really only?)
→ ending → like Speak — snare + high hat

Lullaby: shaker ~~etc~~ more in click part?
— over solo.

Maracas Song: ~~for solo — just double hits?~~
watch entry into solo — double, double, 4.
definitely click in front of second verse

N. Song:

Ceremony: attack

Cymbal one: ~~single str. roll for change. No double hit.~~

Red Crayola: only two hits for jumping part (not 3) on high hat; 3 on ride

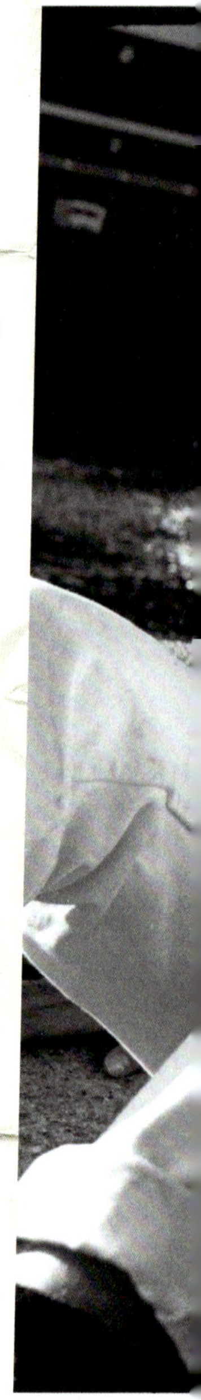

Damon's percussion/drum notes to himself for the *On Fire* session, 1989.

Promo photo by Sergio Huidor, Boston, 1989.

Photos by Sergio Huidor, Boston, 1989.

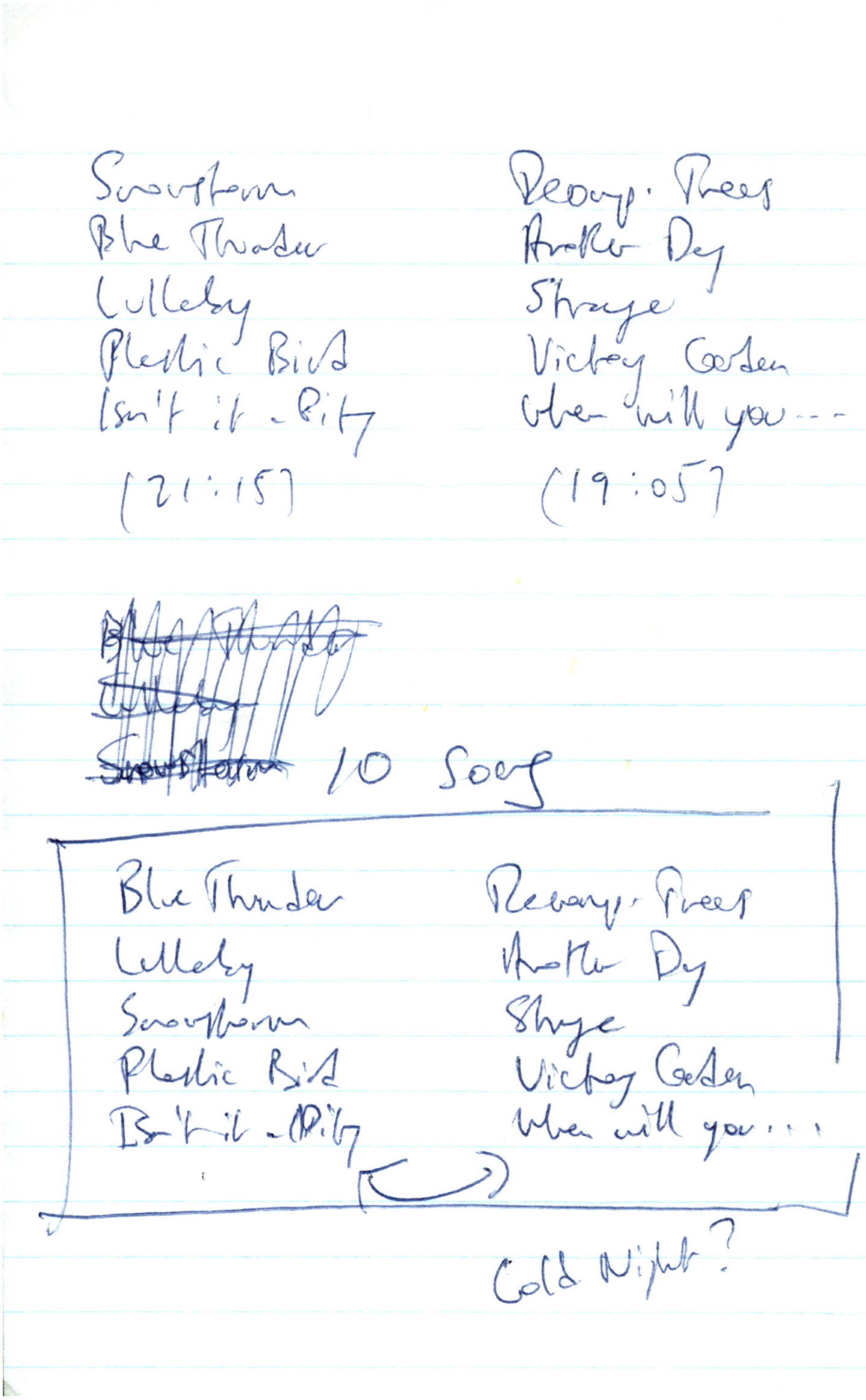
Snowstorm
Blue Thunder
Lullaby
Plastic Bird
Isn't it a Pity
(21:15)

Decomp. Trees
Another Day
Strange
Victory Garden
When will you...
(19:05)

10 Songs

Blue Thunder
Lullaby
Snowstorm
Plastic Bird
Isn't it a Pity

Decomp. Trees
Another Day
Strange
Victory Garden
When will you...

Cold Night?

Working out the track order for *On Fire*, 1989.
Damon's handwriting, Dean's handwriting, and Kramer's input as well.

Strange
~~When Will You Come Home~~
~~Plastic Bird~~
Leave the Planet
Cold Night

~~Blue Thunder~~
~~Decomposing Trees~~
Lullaby
~~Another Day~~
~~Snowstorm~~
Victory Garden
Never get to heaven ←
Maracas
~~C~~eremony
Isn't It a Pity

Happy Song
Disco Song

KRAMER'S ORDER:

Leave the Planet 2:40
Blue Thunder (w/ Sax) 3:45
Plastic Bird 3:20
When will you Come Home 3:20
Snowstorm 5:10
Another Day 3:40
≈ 24:00

Decomposing Trees 4:05
Cold Night 2:35
Lullaby 3:50
Strange 3:15
Victory Garden 2:45
Isn't it a Pity 5:10
≈ 21:00

Ceremony 6:00

Side X	Side Y
Blue Thunder	~~Another Day~~ Decomposing Trees
Snowstorm	Another Day
Lullaby	Victory Garden
Strange	Plastic Bird
Ceremony / Pity	When will You Come Home

10.

Blue Thunder (no sax)	Trees
Lullaby	Another Day
Snowstorm	Victory Garden
Strange	Plastic Bird
COVER	When Will You Come Home

Outtake from *On Fire* cover photo session, Summer 1989.
Again, I set up the photo with my camera and a bulb release and a motor to advance the film. Taken on a hill at the Arnold Arboretum in Jamaica Plain, MA. I wanted it to look like an Elektra album cover from the late 60's, early 70's.

Poster for Shimmy Disc, 1989.

Kramer asked me to design something for his New Music Seminar showcase and I wanted it to feel very '60s—hence the giant daisies. I silkscreened these on our living room floor.

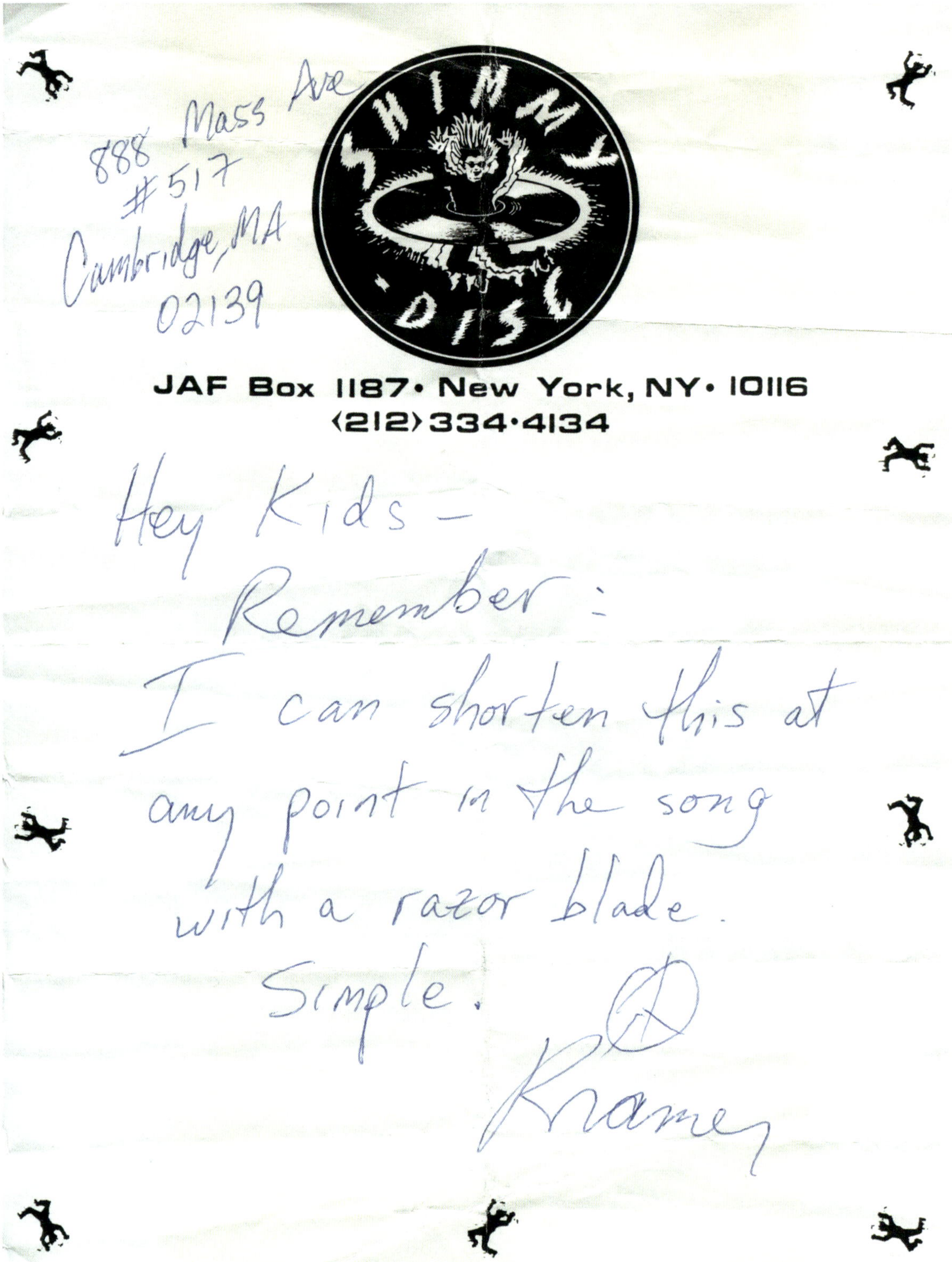

888 Mass Ave
#517
Cambridge, MA
02139

SHIMMY DISC

JAF Box 1187 • New York, NY • 10116
(212) 334•4134

Hey Kids –
Remember:
I can shorten this at any point in the song with a razor blade.
Simple.

Kramer

Note from Kramer, enclosed with a cassette of a mix.

KRAMER: The band was standing on top of a mountain looking down. The first record didn't seem like it got any bad reviews anywhere.

FRANCIS DIMENNO: They accomplished a lot in six short months. They got gigs at the Middle East and T.T. the Bear's, came out with a single and an LP, created a fan base for themselves, got a good deal of mainstream press, and even generated something of a backlash.

TERRY TOLKIN: I was a top salesman and the domestic buyer for Caroline Records wholesalers at the time. I got a test pressing (remember those?) of *Today* just after its release from the label, as a solicitation for me to buy. I got about five a day, and it was already being sold by our competitors, so it took me a couple of weeks to get around to listening to it. In New York City, they had no buzz at all. But the label owner, Marc Alghini, was persistent in calling and finally I got around to listening to it. I loved it immediately but only bought twenty-five copies as it had already been out for a while. We didn't sell out of it for a about a month.

About this time, they came to New York to play their first show here. I had already booked the night at CBGBs for Unrest and some other bands. Hilly Crystal, the owner and operator of CBGBs, called to ask me if I would put Galaxie on the bill. I did and they were great. Looking back now, I'd say they were probably at their zenith. I met Dean that night. I gave them, I think it was about $200—as much as the headliners made. Later on, Mark E. Robinson of Unrest gave them another $100 out of their own money from the show.

MARC ALGHINI: Then it took off. It didn't take long at all before they were playing CBGBs with Sonic Youth! And the *Today* record just starting selling, and it was crazy. I must have made like 5000 copies of that LP, which seemed like a lot; hell, it was a lot for the first album on a tiny label!

MARTIN ASTON: When I found out Dean was born in New Zealand (which made perfect sense), I tried really hard to get Flying Nun UK to release *Today*. But if I remember correctly, Marc Alghini had his sights set higher. They signed to Rough Trade here in the end.

MARC ALGHINI: I always knew that there was no way I was gonna be able to keep them. Everyone has these big dreams. We used to hang out at a kitchenette on Mass Ave.—some diner they turned me on to, that Damon and Naomi went to all the time.

Our deal was structured on a piece of paper. I was going to pay for it, and if they wanted to go to a different label, they'd pay me a percentage.

DEAN WAREHAM: Things can turn ugly so quickly in the music business, especially if you have an unexpected success. I would say it was a little contentious, but it was written right in our contract with Aurora that we had the right to go elsewhere for our second album, and that Marc received a fee if we did so.

DAMON KRUKOWSKI: This is really ancient history!

MARC ALGHINI: The head of Slash Records called me one night all loaded. He yelled at me, telling me I wasn't gonna be able to keep the band, that I was totally screwed. I didn't like that so much.

DAMON KRUKOWSKI: I think that was the first time I ended up playing the management heavy for us. Not a role I enjoyed. It took a lot out of me back then, in fact. But we had no manager, and someone had to do it. Come to think of it, I'm still doing it.

MARC ALGHINI: I was happy they went with Rough Trade—so many people there were true DIY people. They were always upfront and honest with me and abided by my deal with the band. Galaxie were also talking to Slash at the time. Damon and Naomi had a very set vision of where they wanted to go and what they wanted to do.

AUG 30 '89 14:14 FROM ROUGH TRADE INC PAGE.002

ROUGH TRADE

PROMOTIONS AND PUBLICITY

EAST COAST OFFICE
611 BROADWAY
SUITE 536
NEW YORK, NY 10012
212 777-0100
FAX: 212 505-9314

WEST COAST OFFICE
326 SIXTH STREET
SAN FRANCISCO
CALIFORNIA 94103
415 863-9007
FAX: 415 864-6942

AUGUST 28, 1989
FOR IMMEDIATE RELEASE

GALAXIE 500 JOINS ROUGH TRADE LABEL

ROUGH TRADE IS PROUD TO ANNOUNCE THE SIGNING OF BOSTON-BASED TRIO, GALAXIE 500. THE BAND'S FIRST RELEASE ON ROUGH TRADE WILL BE A FULL LP ON FIRE RECORDED AT NOISE NEW YORK, AND PRODUCED BY KRAMER (BONGWATER, BUTTHOLE SURFERS, B.A.L.L.)

THE LP ON FIRE IS SCHEDULED FOR AN OCTOBER 20 RELEASE. THE PROJECT MARKS THE FIRST ROUGH TRADE RECORD TO BE RELEASED SIMULTANEOUSLY ON ALL ROUGH TRADE LABELS WORLDWIDE.

FORMED JUST TWO YEARS AGO, GUITARIST DEANE WAREHAM, DRUMMER DAMON KRUKOWSKI, AND BASSIST NAOMI YANG HAVE CREATED QUITE A FOLLOWING ESPECIALLY IN NEW YORK, AND THROUGHOUT EUROPE. THEIR FIRST RECORD, THE 7" SINGLE "TUGBOAT/KING OF SPAIN" WAS RELEASED IN THE SPRING OF 1988 AND WAS FOLLOWED BY LAST FALL'S LP TODAY, COURTESY OF BOSTON'S INDIE LABEL AURORA. DRUMMER KRUKOWSKI DESCRIBES GALAXIE'S NEW MATERIAL AS "SLOWER, MORE LIVE, AND MORE LUSH."

"This Boston based trio uses a featherlight frame for their music and then fills in the picture with lazy Sunday colors and guitar chords that float over and through the melodies." –CMJ

"GALAXIE 500 will leave your eyes closed contemplating the blissful meadow you discovered when you were eight." –ROCKPOOL

GALAXIE 500 WILL EMBARK ON A EUROPEAN TOUR IN NOVEMBER, AND WILL RETURN TO THE STATES IN TIME FOR A WINTER TOUR OF THE MID-WEST, AND WESTERN STATES TO SUPPORT THE RELEASE OF ON FIRE.

CONTACT:
STEPHANIE BUCCI
NATIONAL PUBLICITY DIRECTOR
JERRY RUBINO
DIRECTOR OF RADIO PROMOTION
212-777-0100

PLEASE REPLY TO:
NEW YORK ☐
SAN FRANCISCO ☐

** TOTAL PAGE.002 **

Rough Trade US announcement of our signing to the label, 1989.

THE BEATLES, 1964
PHOTOGRAPH BY NORMAN PARKINSON

LONDON
15 AUG 1989
S.W.

27p

Dear D&N:

the buzz is moch louder here, and the photos are bigger and glossier. But these weeklies are more than a little ridicolous. I ~~have~~ tried to say as little as possible in the one interview I did, but Im sure there's an attitude to be found somewhere. ~~Simon~~ Roy from SOUNDS asked about the "religious" aspect of the sound just like Bob Biggs. See you very soon. Love, Dean

fotofolio

Krokowski / Yang
888 Massachosetts Ave.
#517
Boston, MA 02139
U.S.A.

Postcard from Dean, Summer, 1989.
Dean went to London for vacation and did some press while he was there.
We had a joke that every journalist in London was named Simon.

DAMON KRUKOWSKI: I remember everything being in sync for *On Fire*—our professional relationship to one another, the band's relationship to Kramer, our feeling for what we could do with a song as a group and on a record. It was exciting, to be making that happen in the studio. It felt like anything we threw into the mix would work.

DEAN WAREHAM: It was recorded in two separate sessions, some as demos for Slash Records, and then the rest right after CMJ or the New Music Seminar. We wanted to finish the album before signing with a label, so there would be no argument about where and how to make it—it would be done already. Anyway, we took our time with this one, spending at least seven days making it, maybe more like ten. Kramer really put on his producer's hat and gave this album a lot more attention.

NAOMI YANG: Making *On Fire* was a very happy experience. I think we were at a point where we were accomplished enough musicians that were able to play what we had in our head. There was a generally optimistic feeling about the direction of the band and we were getting very positive attention from the critics. It was a lot of fun and the possibilities seemed endless, something that I feel I was very lucky to experience. A very joyful, youthful moment.

KRAMER: We made that record so easily! I'm not even sure there were any second takes. It's one of the easiest records I ever made—all the ideas I had, the instruments to play, bringing in Ralph Carney to play, those were all my ideas.

DEAN WAREHAM: I remember Carney asking Kramer what key "Blue Thunder" was in, but Kramer wouldn't tell him. "You'll know," he said.

RALPH CARNEY (*Saxophone on "Blue Thunder" and "Plastic Bird"*): Kramer was recording them and asked me if I wanted to play sax on a tune or two. I said yes. I went to his studio. They were there; they were nice and shy. I played. They liked; it ended up on record—that is the end of the story.

KRAMER: The band was like, "Do what you want, we love what you do." It was like going to a sushi bar with the chef that you know is going to make you happy. The cover was perfect; everything was perfect.

DEAN WAREHAM: Kramer got me to sing some high backing vocals on the first album; on "Oblivious" he slowed the tape down so I could hit the note. I sound like a chipmunk. But it was on the second album that I got it going. There's that part at the end of "Blue Thunder" where I'm singing "I'll drive so far away," but I didn't know beforehand that I was going to sing it so high and loud—it just came out of my mouth that way. I think we were all surprised.

KRAMER: *On Fire*, it's a masterpiece. I love the way they captured this sense of like a longing, a desperation for love and joy, it was a search—the way the music really matched the lyrics.

DEAN WAREHAM: "Strange" is about waiting in line to buy Twinkies at a convenience store on Massachusetts Avenue. I ate Twinkies for dessert (at lunchtime) almost every day when I lived in Boston (at least when I was on a temp job).

My on-again-off-again girlfriend (later my wife) liked me in small doses, but didn't want me getting too serious about her. She lived in New York City, and I would drive down to see her once a month. One particular weekend where she barely gave me the time of day all weekend long (or at any rate that's how I felt), she gave me this shitty yellow plastic toy bird that she had won at the San Gennaro festival in Little Italy, as a parting present, just as I was leaving to drive back to Boston. I was mad at her though; I threw it on the street and stepped on it and wrote an angry song about it, "Plastic Bird."

MICHAEL AZERRAD (*Writer*): The first time I saw Galaxie 500 was at the first Knitting Factory on Houston Street in New York, somewhere around *On Fire*. The thing that struck me right away was Dean's very intense stage presence. He glared out at the audience like that angry teenaged kid in the original Star Trek who would make people disappear by grimacing with his eyes rolling back in his head. Then this elegant throb from Naomi, who was the picture of Zen-like poise in a slo-mo maelstrom. Damon worked up a constant oceanic wash of cymbals, like Elvin Jones or something; he barely seemed to hit the drums and yet clearly drove the music, it was just extraordinary. I knew they were influenced by the Velvet Underground but to me it sounded like Frankie Valli and the Four Seasons doing heavy trank.

NAOMI YANG: At the time, the band was not really a pop sensation, more of a critics' band.

Bio with corrections below

Galaxie 500 are singer/guitarist Dean Wareham, bass player Naomi Yang, and drummer
Damon Krukowski, a rocking trio based in Boston Mass who play slow, lush songs
characterized by long guitar leads, melodic bass lines, and quiet percussion. Their
new album, On Fire, is scheduled for worldwide release by
Rough Trade on October 20, 1989. Produced by Kramer (of Bongwater, B.A.L.L.,
Shockabilly, and Shimmy Disc fame) at his studio Noise New York, the
album is a miraculous combination of sounds from the Velvet Underground and the Beatles,
(1) a fusion of the sixties that only the (1) dawn of the nineties could produce. Like
their first album, Today (released by Boston indie Aurora in October 1988), On Fire is
a collaboration of Kramer's noise, sophistication, and brilliant production, with
Galaxie 500's simple three-chord, half-speed, rave-up sensibilities. But
unlike Today, On Fire finds Dean singing out, the band playing with more assurance, the
(2) songs just as simple but somehow (2) more sure, all captured by Kramer with
a more alive, present sound. Even as the British weeklies declare Today a "classic", On
Fire rushes in to supercede its predecessor, the band cooking, the wax hot. Nine original
(3) tracks, each a potential (3) single, are followed by a cover of George Harrison's "Isn't it a Pity",
epilogue to a weepy album of sometimes spare, sometimes lush, and always melodic love
songs.

Galaxie 500 will be touring England and Northern Europe in November and December,
and the warmer parts of the U.S. in January, in support of their new album release. Their
tour will begin in New York with an appearance at the CMJ convention, October 27th at
(4) CBGB's. A video, of the song "when will you come home" directed by Los Angeles filmaker and artist Sergio Huidor, will also debut
in October.

~~QUOTES FROM PRESS~~

(1) dawn of the nineties could produce.

(2) somehow

(3) potential single

(4) A video of the song "when will you come Home",

Bio written together as a band, 1989.

I have no idea if it was ever used.

GALAXIE 500/STRAITJACKET FITS

Dates many of which t.b.a.

26/9 ICA (G/500 only)
6/11 Kent Uni G/500 only)
8/11 Powerhaus, London
9/11 Boardwalk Manchester
11/11 Academy, London
12/11 Richmond, Brighton
15-19/11 Holland
20/11 Brussels
21/11 Paris
23/11 Lausanne
24/11 Basle
25/11-4/12 Germany
5/12 Camden Palace (G/500)?????
6/12 Manchester Uni
7/12 Riverside, Newcastle
8/12 Glasgow tech
9/12 The Venue, Edinburgh
10/12 Leadmill, Sheffield
11/12 Premises, Norwich
12/12 Duchess of York, Leeds
14/12 Portsmouth Poly
15/12 Subterrania or Borderline, London
19/12 Burburries, Brum.

◂ **First UK and European tour, 1989.**

▴ **Photos from tour travels, 1989.**
These were all taken with my father's old Rolleiflex camera. I loved the square format.

Contact sheets from tour travels, 1989.

ILFORD HP5

Backstage, Thanksgiving Day, Lausanne, 1989.
Photo by Richard Bellia.

Photos by Pat Blashill, New York, 1989.

***Blue Thunder* EP cover, 1990.**
A photo I took at the Jardin de Luxembourg in Paris while we were on tour.

KRAMER: They wanted to be on Shimmy, but I said no. Very much like with [the band] Low, I insisted that they belonged on another label and that this didn't mean I didn't love their music. It meant in fact that I thought they were one of the greatest bands around.

DEAN WAREHAM: We were signed to Rough Trade by Robin Hurley, who ran the American label, and Geoff Travis, who was our A&R man and the head of the company back in England—both great people. It's kind of amazing the list of things he has been involved with: Swell Maps, Jonathan Richman, Shockabilly, to the Smiths, Jesus & Mary Chain, Pulp, the Strokes.

KRAMER: I knew Geoff Travis because he signed Shockabilly. I sent him [*Today*] and he flipped out.

MARC ALGHINI: They took my name off [*Today*] when they got it rereleased by Rough Trade. I was never angry but was definitely hurt. I know what I did and am proud and happy with it. They were a beautiful band.

NAOMI YANG: I loved many of the staff at Rough Trade UK. But in general, I always felt kind of nervous about dealing with record company people. I think I never really felt sure of their kindness being genuine—it felt predicated on our being successful, or perhaps, becoming more successful in the future. In retrospect, I understand how record labels are a business and how a band is an "investment"—but just intuiting that at the time, without really being able to accept the idea of it, made me feel anxious. It was not a friendship, but I was confused by how it looked like a friendship.

DAMON KRUKOWSKI: Geoff was wonderful to talk with about music—he was the one who first told me to listen to the Soft Machine, and Robert Wyatt. He is a Canterbury hippie under that black clothing, you know. And Jeanette Lee was incredible to get to know—Geoff and Jeanette sat opposite each other in the same tiny office, at a partners' desk. It was great to see a woman in that kind of position of authority. It wasn't so common then. Did you know she's the one on the cover of *Flowers of Romance*? What a presence. The whole London office was run by women: Jo Slee, head of production; Pat Bellis, who did international; Chris Stone, our press officer. It was a group of remarkable, independent spirits. Music was always playing, but it wasn't what was on the charts—I heard Sun Ra there for the first time.

TERRY TOLKIN: Galaxie were working on *On Fire* when I came on board [at Rough Trade US]. They were at the epitome of their sound. It's still one of the greatest records of all time. Tensions were mounting, though. Dean and I had become instant best friends immediately. We lived right next to each other.

DAMON KRUKOWSKI: In the US, our luck wasn't nearly as good. The New York office of Rough Trade was a place I didn't like to visit—all the talk was about "units." It was staffed almost entirely by guys. Some had worked previously for majors and all were in the "industry" as a career. I never felt a musical connection there. And then they hired Terry Tolkin, who was divisive from the start. The first time I met Terry he pulled me aside in the office, saying ridiculously flattering things like, I know who the real heart of this band is, blah blah. I thought, who would fall for this?

TERRY TOLKIN: As the A&R man at Rough Trade, I saw that the other two were talented negligibly at best and holding [Dean] back at the worst.

DAMON KRUKOWSKI: Of course, he went on to a high-flown career in the music business. I wasn't surprised at all when Terry was later fired by Geoff. They couldn't have had more different styles.

TERRY TOLKIN: [At Rough Trade], Galaxie 500 was eclipsed by Mazzy Star. And, for some unknown reason one of the worst bands in the world, Souled American, was given untold thousands to "break"—at a time we should have been concentrating on Galaxie 500, Lucinda Williams (instead of suing her), and Scrawl.

KRAMER: Rough Trade put everything into them, and the band was touring constantly—it was the perfect late-'80s mixture of an indie band on an indie label.

Backstage, Germany, 1989.
Photo by John Zielinski.

Backstage, Germany, 1989.
Photo by John Zielinski.

DEAN WAREHAM: We had a UK-based manager for a short time, Craig Taylor, who managed the Chills and also worked with Flying Nun UK. He organized a co-headlining tour (for at least half the tour) with Straightjacket Fits, a band from New Zealand. We spent five weeks, mostly in the UK and Germany, but also playing Holland and Switzerland. Straightjacket Fits rode in the van with the equipment, but we couldn't all fit in there, so we took the train. Kramer came along too. I'll always remember him being amazed when we walked into the Powerhaus in Islington, London, and the club was packed. He was also amazed that we were sleeping on floors instead of in hotel rooms.

DAMON KRUKOWSKI: Our first full UK/European tour was put together by a manager from New Zealand named Craig Taylor, who worked with the Chills. He offered us floors to sleep on, the Chills' van to tour in, and his friends' amps to play on—and then charged us for all of it. We went home with nothing. And Galaxie 500 never worked with a manager again.

DEAN WAREHAM: Being "big" in England wasn't quite real. Things happened much quicker there; they had these national music weeklies that needed to fill their pages with photos and stories about all these young bands. So if they liked you, and John Peel played you on the radio, you could get your picture in the *NME*, and your album might be on the special indie charts (which seemed rather subjective, they varied from one paper to the other).

MARTIN ASTON: The UK press—or elements of it, including myself—championed them. And audiences loved them too. They cast a spell. But what was the biggest show they ever played? Maybe a thousand people? They were never going to break beyond that independent niche at that point. The sound was too slow-dreamy-wild, Dean's vocals way too extreme.

DAMON KRUKOWSKI: It was nice to be liked overseas! Although the tours were grueling, we had a great time in Europe, for the most part. Kramer didn't like vans, so we ended up traveling by train a lot, which felt old-fashioned and romantic—a lot of the trains still had compartments then. I'll never forget the train we took heading out of Berlin, when it was still East Germany. It was all very *Third Man*.

KRAMER: We traveled by train in the UK. I'd suggested that even five minutes driving on the other side of the road on the M1 would turn us into nervous wrecks. So we all got British Rail passes: it was safe and much cheaper, so we were on trains the whole time for our first tour together over there. At one point we were about to leave

London for a gig, and five minutes before the train left, a journalist from *Melody Maker* presented himself on the platform, saying that it was alright, Rough Trade had said this was OK. Now, Damon and Naomi liked everything to be agreed upon weeks in advance, and they didn't like this one bit, but we let him on the train with us. I never saw Naomi in a more foul mood.

This journalist asked us a couple questions and then stopped, said he had other work to do, and he was wondering if you'd fill out this questionnaire for me! So he hands this to us, as though we should be thrilled to do this for him, like it was our pleasure in the first place. Damon looks at this sheet and says "Oh my God." Naomi looks at it and says "Kramer, do mine; do whatever you want just make it as funny as possible," and she goes storming off. I asked her if she was sure, and I was pretty risqué throughout. I saved the clincher for the last question: "If you could choose the manner in which you would die what would it be," and my answer was: "on a pool table." That came out and she didn't talk to me for the rest of the tour.

SIMON RAYMONDE: We invited Galaxie 500 to support the Cocteau Twins in 1991 on our US tour. We'd all been fans for a while, and I first heard them on the John Peel show, maybe around '88.

DEAN WAREHAM: The first Peel Session we did was engineered by Dale "Buffin" Griffin, formerly the drummer in Mott the Hoople. I remember him being impatient. We were amazed at how big the studio was, and this computer they had that could mark the different sections of the song and take the tape machine right to them. It was not Noise New York. And yet, this proves that it is not the equipment itself that matters, but the people twiddling the knobs. My favorite Peel Session recording was our cover of the Sex Pistols' "Submission." People always say that's an unlikely cover, but Damon and I had been playing that one since our days in Speedy & the Castanets; it was one of the first songs we learned together.

NAOMI YANG: I loved being in the BBC studios! It was very exciting to experience the sense of history and the venerable institution of Peel's radio show. It felt like an honor. It didn't seem so hard, as we were used to doing everything very quickly from working with Kramer. But I remember being surprised how different it sounded mixed by someone other than Kramer. I think it made me appreciate even more what Kramer's production had done for our songs.

DAMON KRUKOWSKI: Here's a sentimental memory: Kramer, stoned out of his mind backstage at the Melkweg, Amsterdam, playing us fragments of John Lennon songs on an acoustic guitar, half giggling and halfway to tears. That was a beautiful performance, and only the three of us saw it.

State of the Art, Amsterdam Nov. 18 1989

Everyone had eaten too many hash brownies (except the band) and the band had done too many interviews, and before the show we witnessed the greatest performance, backstage, Kramer with an unplugged guitar, singing bits of songs he loved or hated or both. It was elegiac, and all I could think about was endings, the end. We played slowly, everything we liked playing best then, Kramer was dizzy at the board and joined us for the encores, even Ceremony, which he hated, and Victory Garden, which we did because he loved it. It was the saddest gig ever.

Damon 5.3.90

Damon's Melkweg memories, 1990.
Slipped into a tape box with a live recording of a 1989 show, rediscovered years later while going through live tapes for the Rykodisc reissues.

Manchester, England, 1990.
Photo by Colin Bell.

DEAN WAREHAM: It was funny when Kramer jumped onstage and started playing guitar with us at the Glastonbury Festival—when he was supposed to be out front mixing the live sound.

It was funny when he was searched when we entered the UK from Holland. They told him they had to search him due to trace elements of cannabis they found on his jeans, but it might have been the ponytail and full-length brown leather coat that did it. They had him strip and bend over and all, and then apologized profusely when they didn't find anything.

NAOMI YANG: I think one of my fondest memories of being in the band was when we were opening for the Sundays in England and Harriet lost her voice and cancelled the London show at the last minute. Rough Trade scrambled to get a gig for us in London that night and came up with a pub; I think it was called The Falcon. It was packed, and instead of the big stages that we had been playing with the Sundays we were back to being in our usual atmosphere of a tiny sweaty rock club. It was a really relaxed and completely fun gig—it just felt like we were cut loose from music business responsibilities and could just play music! I guess the music going well was always at the center of my best memories.

DAMON KRUKOWSKI: I always thought the songs changed a lot when we played them live. I guess it was change within a small range. Still, it was the little things that held my attention, night to night.

KRAMER: It bothers me that I never captured the band live—what they were like; it couldn't be done on a regular studio record. Those moments in their sets when they rose up and went to being sometimes as loud as Sonic Youth! It's really too bad we never had the opportunity to do a proper live recording.

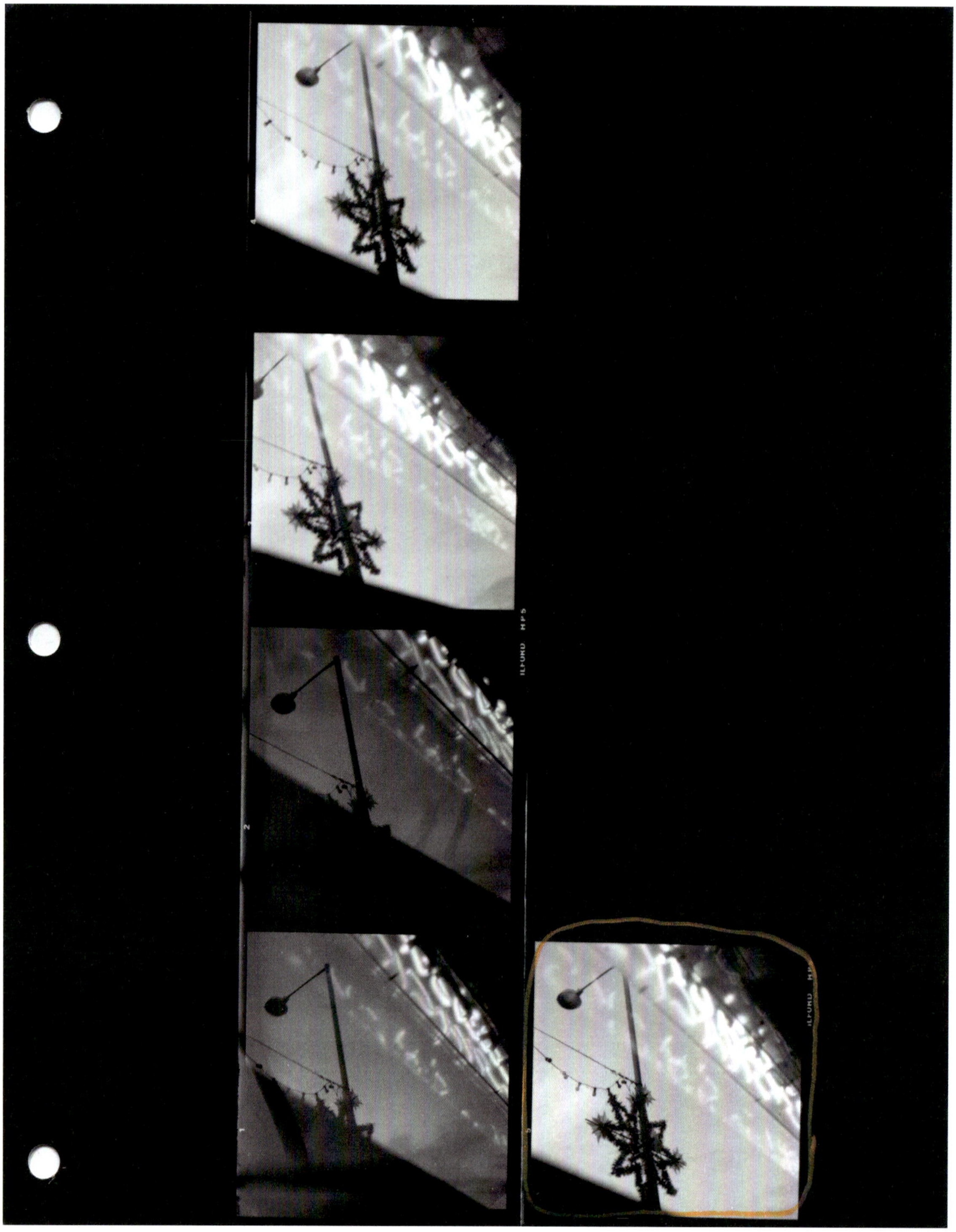

Tour photos, 1989.
I used the circled photo on this page for the back of the **"Fourth of July"** 12" single.

ILFORD HP5
ILFORD HP5
ILFORD HP5

Jan. 5, 1990

Naomi —

Thanks for the shirt... the B.H. shirt you saw was made by Heather, they are long gone. Enclosed is a recent design by me, I hope it is good enough. It's good to hear that Nigel is still active. Did you meet his sister Vanessa? She's a doll.

Hey, your new album is really great. I love the cover and listen to the record often.

We BEAT HAPPENING just recorded a new single. Should be out in March. We will be releasing only singles (here at K) this year: Unrest, Steve Fisk, Pastels, World of Pooh, Thrown-Ups, Mecca Normal, some Velvet Sidewalk, etc. Van and Lee Conner (of Screaming Trees) are recording a single for us with their brother Pat. I've been pretty busy with all this K stuff, don't know when I'll get to tour again. We BEAT HAPPENING are doing some

Box 7154
Olympia, WA 98507
U.S.A.

Letter from Calvin Johnson, 1990.
I still have the shirt he sent me.

shows locally, though. What's next for you guys? You should definitely set up here if you come west, I can get you a bunch of shows. Is Tom still booking you?

Anyway, say hi to the gang for me O.K. bye

love,

Calvin Johnson

(206) 786-1594

Box 7154
Olympia, WA 98507
U.S.A.

VOICE

PAZZ & JOP

FEBRUARY 27, 1990 ● MUSIC SUPPLEMENT ● VOL. 4, NUMBER 1

GALAXIE 500 and the Selves are my bands-that-do-all-the-wrong-things-but-do-it-right. Both bands take from the Velvet Underground (the kiss of death), play half-assed, and are composed of narcoleptics.
ROB O'CONNOR
Jersey City

25 AND UNDER

1. **De La Soul:** *3 Feet High and Rising* (Tommy Boy) .... **333 (28)**
2. **N.W.A.:** *Straight Outta Compton* (Ruthless) ..... **155 (13)**
3. **Beastie Boys:** *Paul's Boutique* (Capitol) .... **107 (10)**
4. **Soul II Soul:** *Keep On Movin'* (Virgin) .... **95 (8)**
5. **Pixies:** *Doolittle* (4AD/Elektra) .... **85 (7)**
6. **Jungle Brothers:** *Done by the Forces of Nature* (Warner Bros.) .... **75 (7)**
7. **Galaxie 500:** *On Fire* (Rough Trade) .... **72 (9)**
8. **Neneh Cherry:** *Raw Like Sushi* (Virgin) .... **66 (6)**
9. **Madonna:** *Like a Prayer* (Sire) .... **63 (4)**
10. **The Bats:** *Daddy's Highway* (Communion) .... **58 (5)**
11. **Queen Latifah:** *Long Live the Queen* (Tommy Boy) **50 (5)**
12. **The Mekons:** *The Mekons Rock 'n' Roll* (A&M) ...... **47 (5)**
13. **Pere Ubu:** *Cloudland* (Fontana) .... **45 (2)**
14. **3rd Bass:** *The Cactus Album* (Def Jam) .... **39 (4)**
    The Frogs: *It's Only Right and Natural* (Homestead) .... **39 (4)**

Clipping from the *Village Voice*, 1990.

ALBUMS

1. **De La Soul:** *3 Feet High and Rising* (Tommy Boy) .... **1050 (89)**
2. **Neil Young:** *Freedom* (Reprise) .... **790 (68)**
3. **Lou Reed:** *New York* (Sire) .... **754 (65)**
4. **The Neville Brothers:** *Yellow Moon* (A&M) .... **621 (57)**
5. **Neneh Cherry:** *Raw Like Sushi* (Virgin) .... **594 (57)**
6. **N.W.A.:** *Straight Outta Compton* (Ruthless) .... **594 (44)**
7. **Elvis Costello:** *Spike* (Warner Bros.) .... **521 (47)**
8. **The Mekons:** *The Mekons Rock 'n' Roll* (A&M) .... **501 (45)**
9. **Soul II Soul:** *Keep On Movin'* (Virgin) .... **460 (39)**
10. **Pixies:** *Doolittle* (4AD/Elektra) .... **416 (38)**
11. **Tom Petty:** *Full Moon Fever* (MCA) .... **381 (35)**
12. **Beastie Boys:** *Paul's Boutique* (Capitol) .... **347 (32)**
13. **Fine Young Cannibals:** *The Raw and the Cooked* (I.R.S.) .... **332 (36)**
14. **Bob Mould:** *Workbook* (Virgin) .... **311 (26)**
15. **Bob Dylan:** *Oh Mercy* (Columbia) .... **295 (31)**
16. **The Replacements:** *Don't Tell a Soul* (Sire) .... **290 (24)**
17. **Pere Ubu:** *Cloudland* (Fontana) .... **283 (24)**
18. **Madonna:** *Like a Prayer* (Sire) .... **235 (22)**
19. **Bonnie Raitt:** *Nick of Time* (Capitol) .... **225 (24)**
20. **Boogie Down Productions:** *Ghetto Music: The Blueprint of Hip Hop* (Jive) .... **203 (19)**
21. **XTC:** *Oranges and Lemons* (Geffen) .... **203 (18)**
22. **Jungle Brothers:** *Done by the Forces of Nature* (Warner Bros.) .... **201 (21)**
23. **Queen Latifah:** *Long Live the Queen* (Tommy Boy) .... **173 (18)**
24. **Roy Orbison:** *Mystery Girl* (Virgin) .... **152 (15)**
25. **Terence Trent D'Arby:** *Neither Fish Nor Flesh* (Columbia) .... **142 (15)**
26. **Kate Bush:** *The Sensual World* (Columbia) .... **141 (15)**
27. **Caetano Veloso:** *Estrangeiro* (Elektra/Musician) .... **139 (12)**
28. **Lyle Lovett:** *Lyle Lovett and His Large Band* (MCA) .... **138 (10)**
29. **Rolling Stones:** *Steel Wheels* (Rolling Stones) .... **137 (16)**
30. **Janet Jackson:** *Rhythm Nation 1814* (A&M) .... **137 (15)**
31. **Galaxie 500:** *On Fire* (Rough Trade) .... **136 (16)**
32. *Batman* (Warner Bros.) .... **124 (14)**
33. **The Jesus and Mary Chain:** *Automatic* (Warner Bros.) .... **123 (14)**
34. **Aerosmith:** *Pump* (Geffen) .... **122 (14)**
35. **Don Henley:** *The End of the Innocence* (Geffen) .... **121 (10)**
36. **Daniel Lanois:** *Acadie* (Opal/Warner Bros.) .... **120 (13)**
37. **Tracy Chapman:** *Crossroads* (Elektra) .... **118 (11)**
38. **Quincy Jones:** *Back on the Block* (Qwest) .... **113 (10)**
39. **The Cure:** *Disintegration* (Elektra) .... **107 (12)**
40. **NRBQ:** *Wild Weekend* (Virgin) .... **107 (10)**

This poll compiles ballots from 255 critics, who divided 100 points among 10 1989 LPs. Points determined placement, with total mentions (indicated in parentheses) used for tie-breaking. Maximum per album: 30. Minimum: 5.

CAFF 9

GALAXIE 500

Rain

Don't Let Our Youth Go To Waste

The Caff Corporation

Spring 1990

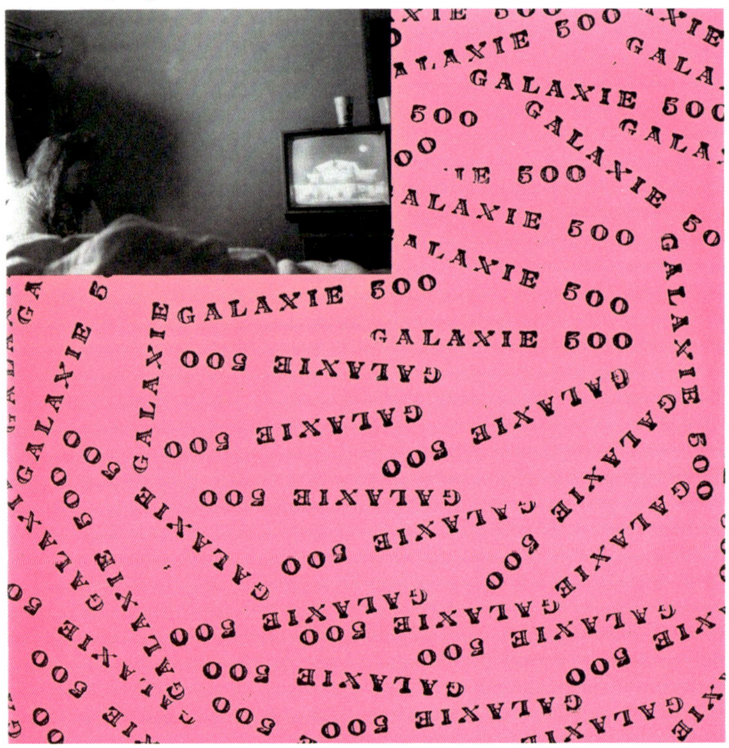

"Rain" 7" single, 1990.

A live recording released by Caff Records (run by Bob Stanley, later of St. Etienne). The photo is of Dave Rick, watching tv in a motel room the four of us shared on tour. I wanted the design to feel like a punk rock flag.

Basement Flat, 61 Dartmouth Park Road,
Tufnell Park, London NW5 1SL.

GALAXIE 500

RAIN / DON'T LET OUR YOUTH GO TO WASTE

Recorded live at CBGB's, New York City
May 13, 1989

with DAVE "magic fingers" RICK and
sound by KRAMER KRAMER KRAMER

pictured: Dave Rick on the road, 1989

RAIN (Lennon/McCartney)

DON'T LET OUR YOUTH
GO TO WASTE (Richman)

Manchester, England, 1990.
Photos by Ian Tilton.

Los Angeles, 1990.

Galaxie
500

Postcard from Calvin Johnson.

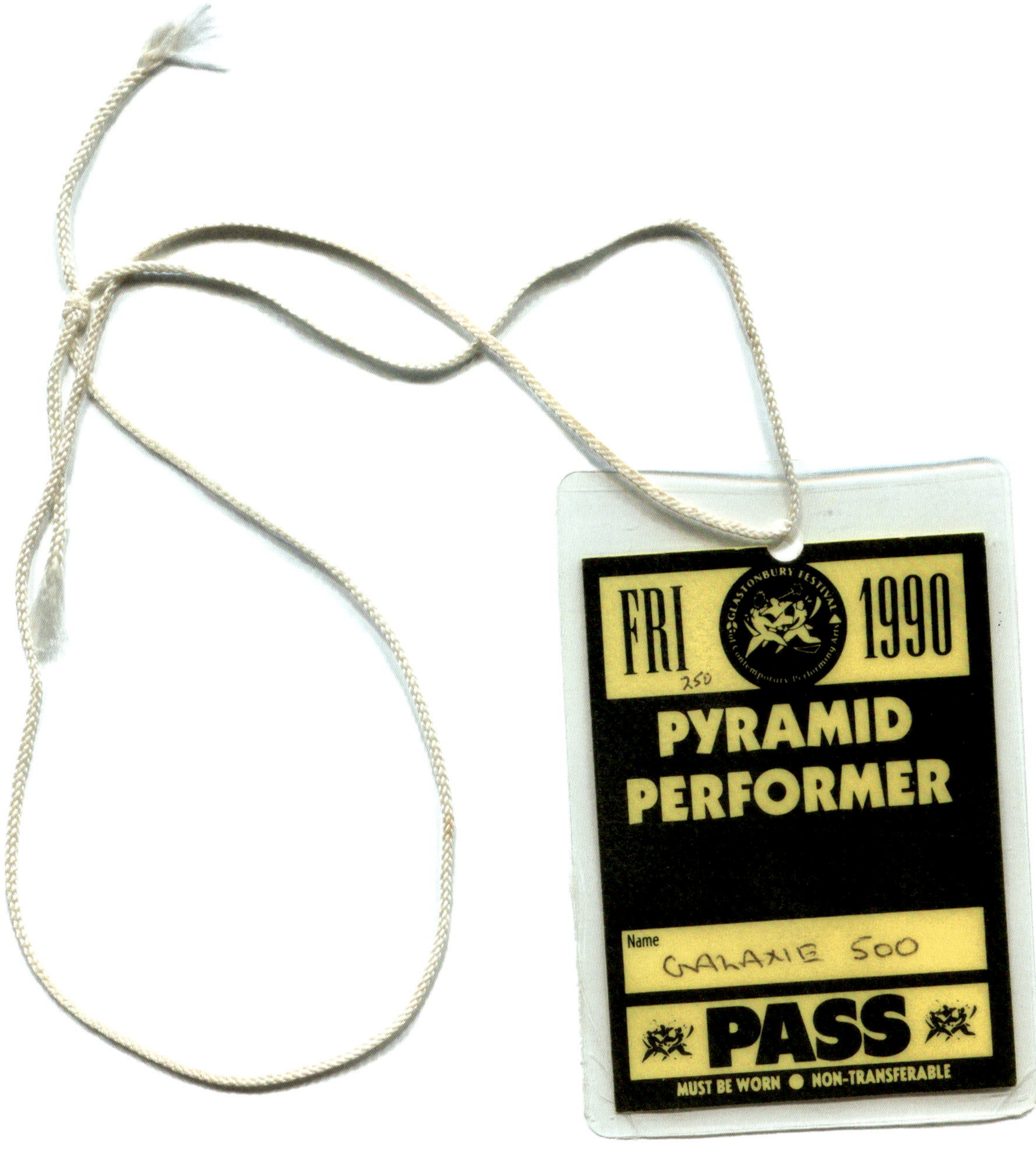

Glastonbury Festival backstage pass, Summer 1990.

Flyer from Bizarre Festival, Germany, and a Polaroid taken nearby on the Rhine, Summer 1990.
The Ramones were in a dressing room/trailer next to ours. We were in the middle of nowhere. Someone came and knocked on their door and delivered pizza. The trailer rocked back and forth as they rehearsed inside. We were delighted.

PROGRAM/ PROGRAMME

TORSDAG/ THURSDAY 28/6

	Ny Blå scene New Blue Stage	Orange scene Orange Stage	Grøn scene Green Stage
17.45	Her Personal Pain (DK)		
18.00			Terminator Ted (DK)
19.15	Les Satellites (F)		
19.30			Del Amitri (UK)
21.00	The Leather Nun (S)		
21.30			Bodeans (USA)
23.00	22-Pistepirkko (SF)		Miss B. Haven (DK)
	Konferencier: Leif Bender		Konferencier: Niels Meilvang

FREDAG/ FRIDAY 29/6

	Ny Blå scene New Blue Stage	Orange scene Orange Stage	Grøn scene Green Stage
12.00			Skan Beat (DK/N/S)
13.30	Gilmartins (DK)		
14.00		Hotel Hunger (DK)	Mekons (UK)
15.00	Mikael Wiehe (S)		
16.00		Philip Boa & The Voodoo Club (D)	Soundgarden (USA)
16.30	Eat (UK)		
18.00		Gorky Park (USSR)	Thåström (S)
19.00	Ry Cooder & David Lindley (USA)		
20.00			The Cramps (USA)
20.30		Midnight Oil (AUS)	
21.00	Melissa Etheridge (USA)		
22.00			TV-2 (DK)
23.00	Mojo Nixon (USA)	Bob Dylan (USA)	
00.30			The The (UK)
01.00	Galaxie 500 (USA)		
01.30		Pretty Maids (DK)	
02.30	Psychotic Youth (S)		Havanna 3 A.M. (UK)
	Konferencier: Leif Bender	Konferencier: Kim Menzer + Svend Rasmussen	Konferencier: Niels Meilvang

Ret til ændringer i musikprogrammet forbeholdes.
The management reserves the right to make any alterations in the programme.

Program from Roskilde Festival, Denmark, Summer 1990.

Promo photos by Sergio Huidor, Boston, 1990.

This is Our Music album cover, 1990.

DEAN WAREHAM: Right before we recorded our third album in 1990, I was able to quit my day job—doing typing and other office work at Brigham and Women's Hospital and then at an engineering firm across from the Government Center. We weren't exactly getting rich off the band, but our expenses were pretty minimal. We were living the dream, at least I know I was; this was more than I had thought possible. We were on MTV (Sunday nights after midnight).

CHRIS XEFOS: I did sound for Galaxie 500 a few times during '89 and '90, at gigs in New York mostly. I didn't feel like I really started hanging out with them until the tour in October '90. They were doing this European-style tour in the US, flying to each city and using backline at every gig, and they asked me to come along to do sound. I was very excited to be asked along, and it was a great time (for me). During that tour I had kinda seen the two camps (Dean vs. Damon/Naomi) happening. Damon really took care of all the details during that tour, and I saw him get really "New York" on people's asses at points. It was an interesting side to see, Damon as the "protector."

DAMON KRUKOWSKI: By the time the band was earning our living I don't remember it as a dream at all. By then everything had become something of a nightmare. The more money we earned, the less I recognized Dean for the friend I once had. And the creepier I found the people around him, Terry Tolkin in particular.

NAOMI YANG: Dean had made his unhappiness clear, but we were unhappy with him too. It seemed like Dean was very much thinking only about himself. He even mentioned to us that he had to do certain things on his own because he had to think about his own career after the band. Meanwhile, Damon and I were still putting all our efforts into Galaxie 500's music and success of the band. Maybe the three of us didn't have the tools to work things out, but there certainly also were a lot of outside forces, people who were happy to divide the band, pulling us apart.

TERRY TOLKIN: By the time *This Is Our Music* came along they hated each other. I walked into some ugly scenes at Noise New York during those sessions, so I avoided them. It's my least favorite Galaxie 500 record. I never listen to it; I like the other two.

DAMON KRUKOWSKI: Oh please, you think Dean was the only unhappy one in the group? You try being in a band with him.

NAOMI YANG: We weren't in different cities until we were making the third record. Dean lived in Boston up until then, but his girlfriend was in New York and he wanted to move back. Damon and I were still in graduate school in Cambridge at the time. It was difficult on the songwriting—we had always each brought in riffs, but now there weren't the weekly rehearsals to hash them out. I think the songs had less time to develop together before we recorded them, a process I really missed.

DEAN WAREHAM: For the first couple of years we were all in Boston. Then, after we finished *On Fire*, I moved in with my girlfriend in New York, but still had a room at my friends' place in Jamaica Plain, Boston. I spent a lot of time driving back and forth between Boston and New York, and sometimes that worked but sometimes it was a pain in the ass.

NAOMI YANG: Recording *This Is Our Music* was a terrible, sad, and angry time. Noise New York was literally falling apart—the fire department had come in and told Kramer that the wall to the mixing booth was a fire hazard and he had to tear it down, so it was just rubble. Damon and I were feeling very betrayed by Dean because it became clear he was doing solo projects without telling us.

KRAMER: They were kind of breaking up at this point, but there are some great songs on there. I knew it could have been twice as good as it was.

Damon and Naomi had really taken over an executive aspect in which they scrutinized the things I wanted to do and asked for changes. Up until then I did exactly what I wanted to do—it really was like I was the fourth member of the band. When we toured together live, which I did right up to the Cocteau Twins tour, it was the same way.

DAMON KRUKOWSKI: Dean's attitude was horrendous at that point."I can't be bothered," was his catch phrase, I remember; he applied it to everything from lunch to overdubs. I even had to finish one of his lyrics for him; he'd run out of them and seemed to have stopped trying. All he had left was this line, "I'm sorry about your goldfish," and here we had this lovely tune already down on tape, going to waste. I thought, well I know what I'm sorry about, so I wrote it on that theme and gave it to him.

DEAN WAREHAM: We probably rushed into making the final record. Some of it is vintage Galaxie 500—like "Fourth of July" and "Listen the Snow is Falling" and "Hearing Voices." But we could have used some more songs, and things were tense in the studio, and elsewhere, it seemed we were arguing a lot about ridiculous things. Kramer even tried to have us record some of our parts at different times—to get away from this feeling that all three of us needed to be there in the studio for every single note that went to tape. But this idea didn't really pan out.

KAREN SCHOEMER (*Writer*): My favorite song was "Fourth of July." Its rhythm was liquid. It spoke of apathy and inertia, of being alienated from the action. The 80s, Wall Street greed, Reagan, Bush dad, stadium rock were happening on the horizon and

FOR IMMEDIATE RELEASE

Damon Krukowski, drummer with the much touted Rough Trade recording artists GALAXIE 500, has cut his hair. His old look has "gone the way of the vinyl LP" said Krukowski, reached by telephone this weekend at his New England retreat. "It's a commercial move as well as an aesthetic one" said the sensible Krukowski, adding, "our new single is poised to kill in the charts, and this might give it the kick it needs."

For more information contact Chris Stone at 01-837-6747.

♡ from Damon

Fake press release, 1990.

Damon wrote this as a joke because it was the sort of thing we would read all the time in the British press. He sent it to the publicist at Rough Trade, thinking it would make her laugh. But she didn't realize he was kidding and dutifully sent it out. No one picked it up.

we were all ignoring it, trying to make our own world, trying to pull the shades so we didn't have to see the sky. It worked for a while. It was a beautiful time.

NAOMI YANG: For us, all our energy was put into the communal effort, and it was very confusing that Dean didn't feel that way too. When we played the album for Rough Trade, Geoff Travis told us he thought we needed to go back in the studio. Damon, Kramer and I all agreed, but Dean refused. Things were that bad.

DAMON KRUKOWSKI: It was kind of shocking, because none of us had ever contradicted Geoff to his face; he was like our boss. We were all sitting in Geoff and Jeanette's little office together, Kramer was with us too, and Dean and Geoff were at odds. I remember thinking, ah, thank you Geoff. Naomi and I were eager to get back in the studio, for patches to leads and other things that I think we all knew could be better. It's not that I don't like the record that resulted; I'm very proud of it, and in a lot of ways I think it was a huge step forward for us musically—in our songwriting and in our arranging.

KRAMER: Damon and Naomi took over the sequencing for *This Is Our Music*. It's a far inferior record. There were three amazing songs that Damon and Naomi decided not to be on the record. They were really taking...I was producing, but they were asking for changes.

DAMON KRUKOWSKI: Now I can see the band was done. I hated Dean at the time for the way he ended it, which I thought was cowardly, and why. He was making a move for the major-label contract we were being offered on his own, instead of together, which I thought was low. But I don't think he was so wrong to end it. It was time to move on, for all of us.

PHIL McMULLEN: I met and interviewed Galaxie 500 during the ninth date of what turned out to be their final European tour, in November 1990. They played in Bristol, South West England, and were there to promote their then new album *This Is Our Music*. What I hadn't realized when I walked into the dingy little dressing room the band had been allocated, was that here was a band at crisis point. They were barely talking to one another, let alone to journalists.

"How would you describe your music?" I asked. "It's bollocks," replied Dean. Thanks, Dean. Naomi was more circumspect, and came out with what I felt was the most telling remark of the whole evening. "People always ask me why I don't smile on stage. Why should I, though? There's nothing especially cheerful going on up there..."

TERRY TOLKIN: After the *On Fire* tour [Dean] started talking about how unhappy he was in the band. He was constantly being voted out by the rhythm section, but he had all of the ideas.

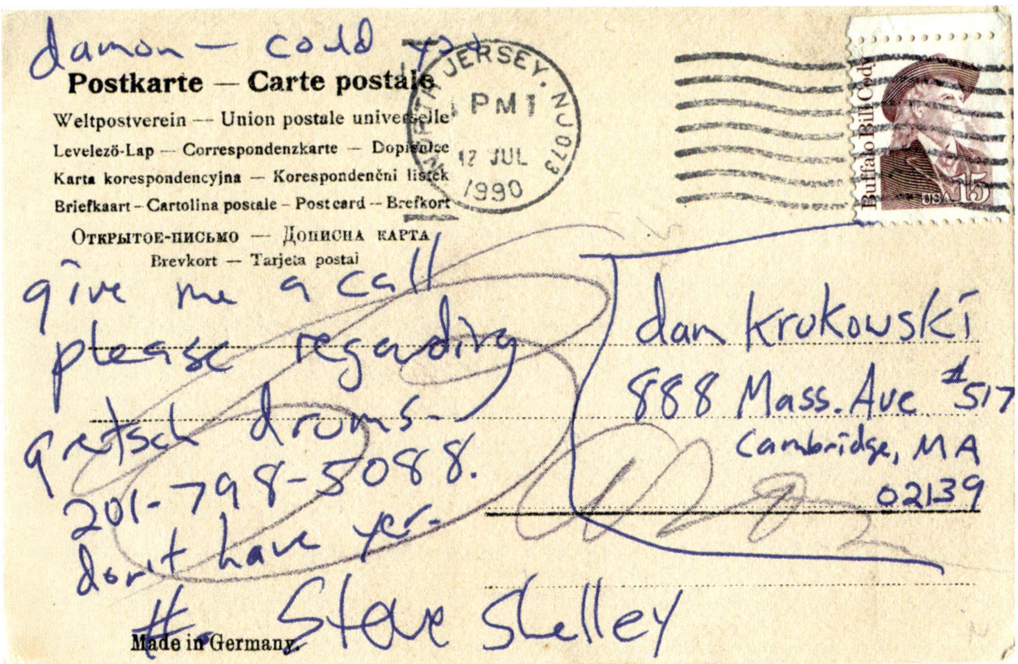

Postcard from Steve Shelley of Sonic Youth to Damon, re: Gretsch drums, 1990.

Outtakes from *This Is Our Music* cover photo session by Norman Gholson von Holtzendorff, Los Angeles, Summer 1990. Norman was another friend of mine from college. We did this photo shoot on the roof of his apartment building; most of the clothes and props were his, and he did the styling as well.

VIRTUE

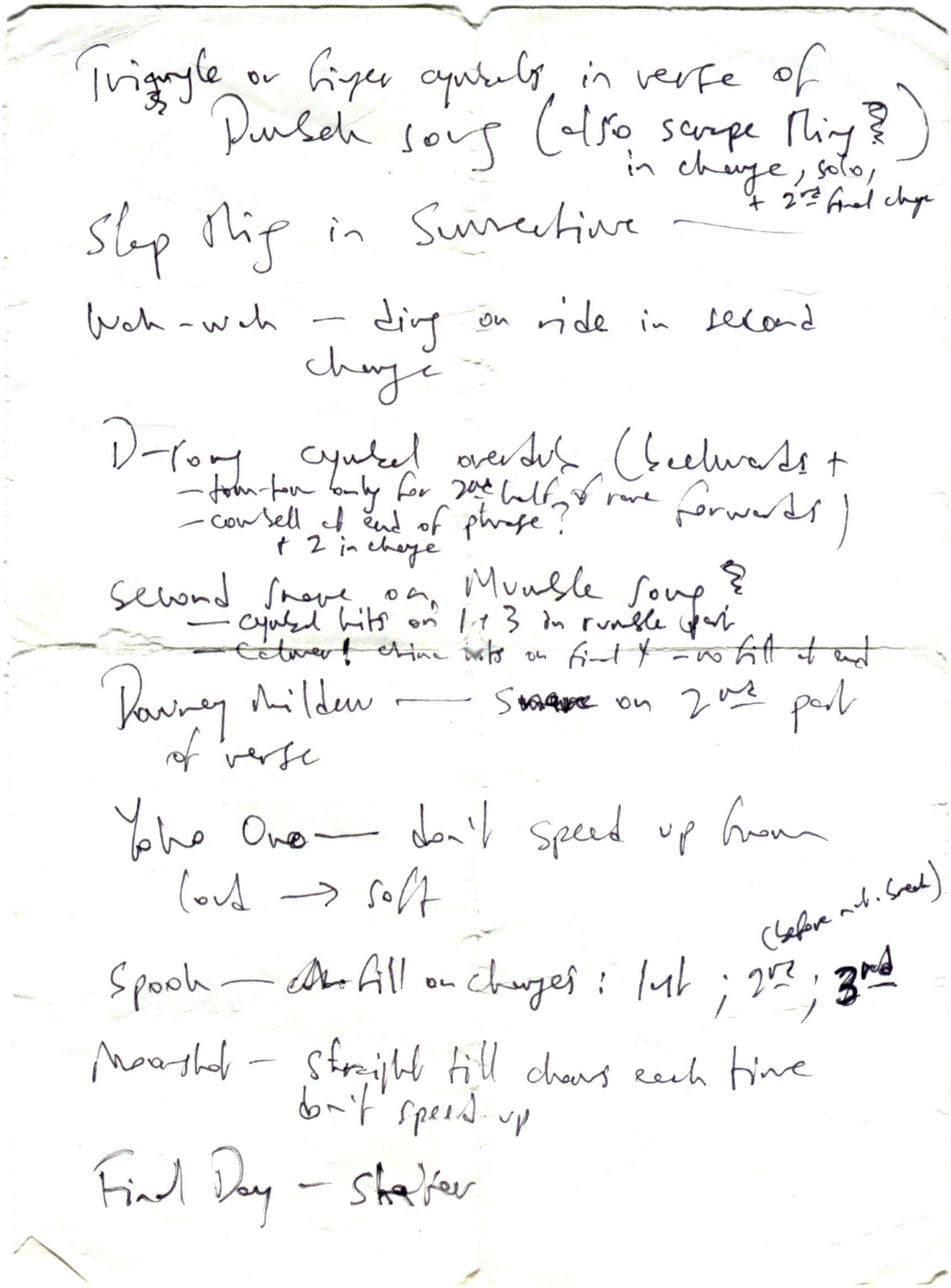

Triangle or finger cymbals in verse of
Dunbeck song (also scrape thing?)
in change, solo,
+ 2nd final change

Slap thing in Surrective —

Wah-wah — ding on ride in second
change

D-rone cymbal overdub (backwards +
forwards)
- tom-tom only for 2nd half, & more
- cowbell at end of phrase?
+ 2 in change

Second snare on Mumble song?
— cymbal hits on 1 + 3 in rumble part
— ~~Cobweb! china hits on final X — no fill at end~~

Rainy Mildew — S~~nare~~ on 2nd part
of verse

Yoko Ono — don't speed up from
loud → soft

Spook — ~~[illegible]~~ fill on changes: 1st; 2nd; 3rd
(before mid. break)

Moonshot — straight till chorus each time
don't speed up

Final Day — Shaker

Damon's percussion notes from *This Is Our Music* recording session, Summer 1990.

Photos by Sergio Huidor, Boston, 1990.
I always liked how you can see Sergio's reflection in the top left photo, on the far right of the image. He was using my Rolleiflex and is looking down at the ground glass to frame the photo.

Promo photo by Michael Lavine, New York, 1990.

Outtakes from photo session by Michael Lavine, 1990.

Outtakes from photo session by Michael Lavine, 1990.

Damon & Naomi — so you have same idea! See you very very very soon — Love Cx.

GALAXIE 500 Interview schedule September 1990

Monday, 24th 081·950·5489 Raymond Coffer Son: Nicholas

11am Melody Maker photo session with Phil Nichols @ Albion Studio, 17a Balfe St., N1 (behind Malt & Hops).

1pm City Limits interview with Mark Sinker.

2pm TLN(Glasgow What's On) phoner with Innes Reekie.

2.30pm Brumbeat/What's On phoner with Mike Davies.

3pm Lime Lizard photosession with Richard.

3.30pm Lime Lizard interview with Clive Gabriel.

4.30pm Liberation - Lydie Barbarian.

5.30pm Outlook — Patrick

Tuesday, 25th

~~11am TOP magazine interview with Pete Clarke.~~

12.15pm Sheffield Telegraph - phoner with Martin Lilliker

12.45pm Radio Sheffield - phoner with Kris Vigar.

1.15pm Italian/Yugo press - Sasha Stojanovic

2pm ~~NME~~? 2.30 — Peter S. 370·6701 Rm. 104

~~3pm~~ 2.30 Rec. Mirror

3.30pm Fatea fanzine interview with Neil King (phoner).

4pm Melody Maker interview with Ian Gittins.

5.30pm ~~NME~~?

8pm No 1 Party!!!!!

Wednesday, 26th

11am Transmission (TV) with Rachel Davies @ 30 Market Pl. W1.

12.30pm Multi-track 3 (BBC World Service) interview with Richard Arran @ Centre Block, Bush House, The Strand, WC2.

1

UK press schedule, Fall 1990.

"Fourth of July" 12" single, 1990.
Another tour photo, this one taken in London.

Ad for "Fourth of July" single, Fall 1990.

NME

"Fourth of July"
Galaxie 500

Well this single is o.k., I mean to say it is brilliant in an o.k. manner, not in a brilliant brilliant manner but that's o.k. Of course it _is_ brilliant, but for a brilliant band that's just o.k., isn't it? The brilliant b-side is unfortunately a cover of an o.k. song; or was it an o.k. cover of a brilliant song? The album should be better, or, worse.

Damon's prediction for the NME review of the "Fourth of July" single.
You can tell we're getting jaded.

Photo session at my parents' house, New York, Summer 1990.
Went back to the "self-portrait" style of our first promo photos and took these myself.
My favorite is the one of just Damon and Dean.

Galaxie 500 Fall Tour Dates

Date	Venue	Contact
Wed 10/10 – 750 vs 50%	Paradise Rock Club 12-18 guest list 967 Commonwealth Avenue Sc: 5 p. Boston, MA (617) 254-2054 Tim McKenna 9:15 set	Pam Martin Don Law Company 36 Bay State Road Cambridge, MA 02138 (617) 547-0620
Thur. 10/11	The Point 420 Moreland Ave. 6:30 load-in 404·577·4377 874·5558 FAX	DAN NOLAN 404·876·8436
Fri 10/12 – $1000 ✓	Lounge AX 2438 North Lincoln Avenue Chicago, IL 60614 (312) 463-5926 (312) 348·5317 fax 6 load-in	Sue Miller c/o Lounge AX 2438 North Lincoln Avenue Chicago, IL 60614 (312) 463-5926
Sat 10/13 – $750 ✓	7th Street Entry 29 North 7th Street Minneapolis, MN (612) 338-8388 Jules 5 load-in mid. set	Steve McClellan Loop Station — First Avenue P.O. Box 2126 Minneapolis, MN 55402 (612) 338-8407 FAX (612) 338·5162 "First Avenue"
Mon 10/15 – $1500 ✓	Kennel Club 628 Divisadero San Francisco, CA 94117 (415) 931-9858 *call Jörg 5 pm load-in	Rina Neiman — Jörg c/o Kennel Club 628 Divisadero San Francisco, CA 94117 (415) 931-9858 Fax (415) 863·4305 — att: Jörg at "Nightbreak"
Tue 10/16 – $150 ✓	San Diego ~~TBA~~ The Casbah 2812 Kettner Blvd. (close to airport) 619·294–9033	Harlan 619·286·6958 277·0968 fax
Wed 10/17 – $1000 ✓	~~Hollywood Live~~ ~~6840 Hollywood Blvd~~ ~~Hollywood, CA~~ CONDEMNED (213) 461-6222 Kevin Lyman 714·626·4245 626·6004 fax	Gary Tovar/Paul Tollett Goldenvoice 18811 Huntington Street Suite 240 Huntington Beach, CA 92648 (714) 841-3113 FAX: 714·847·5244
Fri 10/19 – EST: 1000 (✓)	CBGB & OMFUG 315 Bowery New York, NY 10003 (212) 254-0983	Louise Parnassa c/o CBGB & OMFUG 315 Bowery New York, NY 10003 (212) 254-0983 212·995·0019 FAX
Sat 10/20 – $1000 ✓	9:30 Club 9:30 F Street N.W. Washington, D.C. 20004 (202) 393-0930 Simone — 202·638·2008 638·3842 Fax 6 load-in S. check 7p Set. 12p.	Seth Hurwitz c/o 9:30 Club 9:30 F Street N.W. Washington, D.C. 20004 (202) 363-5277

TwinTowers Touring 611 Broadway Suite 616 New York, NY 10012 PH# (212) 995-0649/0650 fax (212) 979-1428

US tour dates, Fall 1990.

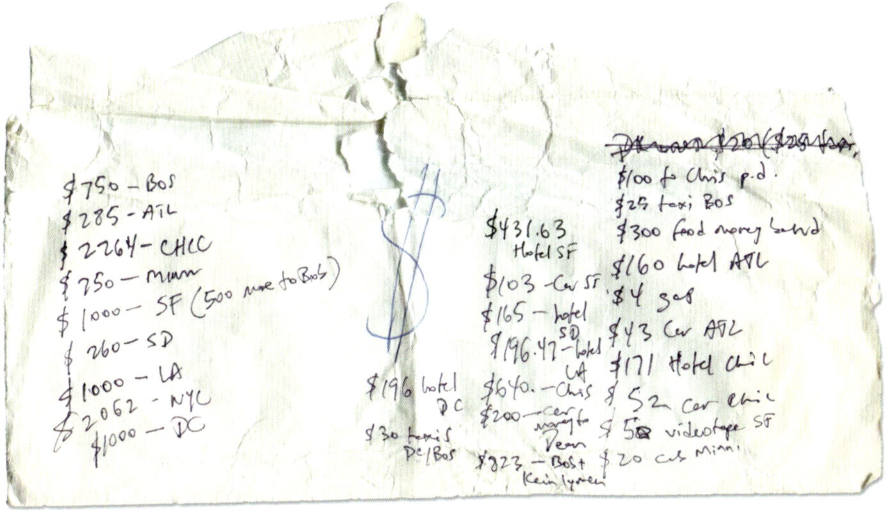

above **The "money envelope" from the US tour, Fall 1990.**

below **Poster, Minneapolis, Fall 1990.**
I liked how they used the exploitation movie theme on this poster—it was so unlike our usual image.

CBGBs ad, Fall 1990.
I thought this was a great bill we had put together—all bands with women in them, much more unusual at the time than it is now.

Photos by O., San Diego, 1990.
O. turned up at every Southern California gig. He was a photographer for *Transworld Skateboarding*—
we were amused that he seemed to like our slow music so much.

San Diego, 1990.
Photos by O.

© Photo by Q.

GALAXIE 500 MUSICIANS

NAOMI: We were hanging out in Boston. We were suffering in graduate school. I was studying architecture, losing my mind. I couldn't take all those damn straight lines. They were looking for a bassist. I dropped out.

DAMON: Dean and I were playing in a band at Harvard while studying comparative literature. We were awful.

DEAN: So I started word-processing as a temp. Actually, I was subverting the temp world.

NAOMI: He was an existential temp. He wore only black to work.

DAMON: We all started playing together in New York. In fact, we had the name before we had the band. We never had a real Galaxie 500, but we rode in one once. And a drug dealer in Washington, D.C., had one.

NAOMI: A drug dealer/private detective.

DEAN: He wanted to trade his car for our Datsun station wagon.

DAMON: I suspect people on the street knew what his car looked like and he wanted to get rid of it.

NAOMI: But we felt it best to keep away from the literal meaning of the name.

DAMON: Besides, we were inspired by lots of stuff.

DEAN: Like, it doesn't bother me to be compared to the Velvet Underground. They're my favorite band of all time. We write all our music together. Nobody walks in with a finished song. On the new record it's easier to understand my lyrics. Our title *This Is Our Music* is stolen from an old Ornette Coleman album. I've never heard it, but I liked the title.

The record's going to take off. We played a festival in England where 500 people were arrested and there were clashes with the police after it happened. We were thankful they didn't throw mud at us. We were warned they like to throw mud.

DAMON: If they like you or if they hate you. It doesn't matter.

DEAN: Though it's fun to walk the line and play an indifferent set, one where the crowd can't make up its mind whether it's a good song or a bad song. Though you can't do that all the time.

DAMON: Just in case, there's a Yoko Ono song on the record.

NAOMI: For commerciality.

DAMON: We love our crowds.

NAOMI: That'll calm them.

AS TOLD TO **WILL DANA**
PHOTOGRAPHY BY **MICHAEL LAVINE**

Interview in *Egg*, 1990.
Photo by Michael Lavine.
Michael had Dean stand on a milk crate, making him tower over Damon and me…the beginning of the end?

egg

P.S. AND THIS IS IMPORTANT:
DAMON...SORRY I CAME ONSTAGE
EARLY AT GLASTONBURY. I WAS WRON
DON'T KNOW WHAT I WAS THINKIN
ALSO NOT TERRIBLEY SURE I REALL
OUGHT TO COME ONSTAGE WITH YOU.
I WAS REALLY PISSED AT THAT U.K
REVIEW THAT HAD A PICTURE OF ME
NEXT TO THE REVIEW OF YOUR GIG.
WE SHOULD DO OUR UTMOST TO KEEP
THAT SHIT FROM HAPPENING AGAIN.
FOR AS MUCH AS I LOVE PLAYING WI
YOU GUYS LIVE, I THINK THE BAND I
INFINITELY MORE IMPORTANT THAN A F
MOMENTS OF PERSONAL PLEASURE FOR ME.

SHIMMY · DISC

JAF Box 1187 • New York, NY • 10116
(212) 334-4134
Fax: (212) 334-3207

HI DAMON...HI NAOMI...

I THINK THE PROBLEMS YOU HAVE WITH THE TEST PRESSING ARE JUST THE TEST. REMEMBER, THE TESTS ARE RUN IN THE MORNING BEFORE THE PRESSES ARE HOT, SO A BIT OF NOI IS TO BE EXPECTED. THERE IS NO WAY IN HELL THAT ANY REAL PROBLEM WOULD HAVE BEEN OVERLOOKED BY THE GREAT JIM SHELTON. TRUST ME ON THIS. JIM IS A PROFESSIONAL. IF YOU HEARD DISTORTION AT HIGH VOLUMES, THAT SOUNDS LIKE AN AMP PROBLEM TO ME, AS MOST AMPS WILL GET A BIT NOISIER AT THE TOP OF THE OUTPUT RANGE. DON'T CONCERN YOURSELF WITH IT AT ALL.

NOW TO THE SLIGHTLY MORE TOUCHY AREA OF [illegible] NOVEMBER. I UNDERSTAND THAT I WAS NEVER ASKED TO ACCOMPANY YOU ON THIS TOUR, AND I SENSE THAT TO BE A DETERIORATION OF SORTS WHICH I FEEL I MUST TRY TO REPAIR. SURELY YOU MUST KNOW THAT LEAVING THE LIVE SOUND UP TO SOMEONE WHO HASN'T A CLUE CAN BE A DANGEROUS MOVE, BUT THERE ARE BIGGER ISSUES AT HAND. IT IS AGAINST MY NATURE TO "BEG" TO COME ALONG, AS GENERALLY , I ONLY WISH TO BE WORKING WITH PEOPLE WHO REALLY WANT TO WORK WITH ME. SOMETHING TELLS ME THAT YOU DO WISH I COULD COME, BUT THAT YOU FEAR MY WORSENING DISPOSITION, KNOWING THAT A MONTH-LONG TOUR CAN ONLY SUCCEED IF CONDITIONS ARE COMFORTABLE, BOTH PHYSICALLY AND MENTALLY. SO NOW TO MY LAME EXCUSE FOR ONE OR TWO MINOR EMOTIONAL OUTBURSTS I FEEL I HAD ON OUR LAST TRIP. I KNOW THIS MAY BE DIFFICULT FOR YOU TO COMPREHEND FULLY, BUT I ALSO KNOW THAT YOU'VE READ ENOUGH NOVELS TO KNOW WHAT DRUG ADDICTION IS. EVEN THOUGH BEING WITHOUT THE SMOKE IS A MAJOR TRIUMPH FOR ME, GETTING TO THAT POINT WAS THE MOST DIFFICULT THING I HAVE EVER TRIED TO DO, AND I DEFINITELY STEPPED ON A FEW PEOPLE IN THE PROCESS, WHILE IN A STATE OF CONFUSION. LIKE ALCOHOL, THE SMOKE WAS DEBILITATING, AND I AM SURE THAT, ON A MORE SUBCONCIOUS LEVEL, I WILL CONTINUE TO DEAL WITH THIS FOR SOME TIME. SURELY YOU MUST HAVE NOTICED A DIFFERENCE BETWEEN THE TIME IN EUROPE AND THE TIME SHORTLY THEREAFTER IN THE STUDIO, WHERE I CANNOT RECALL ANYTHIN BUT GOOD CHEER BETWEEN US, ALL OF US. I CERTAINLY SAW A MARKED IMPROVEMENT. I GUESS, THOUGH THIS ISN'T EASY TO SAY, THAT I NEED YOU GUYS TO STICK WITH ME ON THIS TOUGH ROAD, AND BE DIFFERENT FROM OTHERS WHO ARE SO EASY AND QUICK TO JUDGE ON SO MANY LEVELS. I TREASURE YOUR FRIENDSHIP AS STRONGLY AS I TREASURE OUR WORKING RELATIONSHIP, AND IF i'm NOT GONNA GO WITH YOU IN NOVEMBER IT'D BE HEARTWARMING TO HEAR THAT THE REASONS ARE SOLELY FINANCIAL AND NOT FROM A FEAR OF THE FUTURE, WHICH I CONSIDER BRIGHT AND RADIANT. I REALLY AM SORRY THAT I GOT CRANKY OVER THERE, AND I WOULDN'T SAY THAT IF I DIDN'T MEAN IT. I KNOW I GOOFED UP A FEW TIMES. WE ALL FUCK UP EVERY NO AND THEN, BUT CONSIDERING THIS WAS A RESULT OF 16 YEARS OF DRUGS AND STUPIDITY, I THINK I'M O.K. OH YEAH, REMEMBER WHEN YOU GUYS WERE IN THE ROUGH AND I WAS TRYING TO CHAT IT OUT WITH YOU, WELL I JUST THOUGHT I WAS HELPING, BUT MY THOUGHT PROCESSES WERE FUCKED, SO I'M UNSURE (IN RETROSPECT OF WHAT I WAS DOING. BE ASSURED THAT I WON'T GET INVOLVED WITH BAND STUFF UNLESS IT RELATES TO UND, OR UNLESS I'M ASKED FOR ADVISE. I REALLY WANT THIS TO BE THE ONE WORKING RELATIONSHIP I C SUCCESS ON ALL LEVELS. I'D LIKE TO GO WITH YOU IN NOVEMBER IF YOU'LL HAVE ME. I'LL WOR AND NOT ONLY THAT, I WON'T FART ON THE TRAIN.

Love ☮ Kramer

Fax from Kramer, 1990.
The last time we had taken him on tour as soundman had been very difficult…

Dear Kramer —

Thanks for your fax. I think you're really right when you say we want you to be there, we're just a little nervous. Maybe we can talk on the phone about it, or in New York. Anyway you know it's hard for us to think about someone else doing the sound; right now I'm calling England, travel agent, etc., to put the whole budget together so we can give you an answer quickly.

(Say.... how cheap was it you said you'd work?)

You sure you're ready for 4 weeks of our sound?

♡ DK

Damon's fax back to Kramer.

:OM FAIRWARNING AGENCY 10.18.1990 15:37 P. 2

FairWarning

GALAXIE 500

NOVEMBER	THU	1	NEWCASTLE, Riverside
	FRI	2	EDINBURGH, Venue
	SAT	3	GLASGOW, College of Building & Printing
	SUN	4	DUNDEE, Dance Factory
	MON	5	OFF (Liverpool reservations)
	TUE	6	LIVERPOOL, Polytechnic
	WED	7	LEICESTER, University
	THU	8	OFF (Tower in London)
	FRI	9	NORWICH, Waterfront
	SAT	10	SHEFFIELD, Leadmill
	SUN	11	BRISTOL, Bierkeller
	MON	12	OFF (London reservations)
	TUE	13	BIRMINGHAM, Goldwyns
	WED	14	MANCHESTER, International I
	THU	15	LONDON, University of London Union
	Channel crossing 16th		
NOVEMBER	SAT	17	RENNES, L'Ubu
	SUN PARIS		
	MON	19	PARIS, New Morning
	TUE	20	AMIENS, La Lune Des Pirates
	WED	21	BRUSSELS, Vaartkapoen
	THU	22	AMSTERDAM, Paradiso
	FRI DUSSELDORF		
	SAT	24	DUSSELDORF, Philipshalle
	SUN FRANKFURT		
	MON	26	FRANKFURT, Batschkapp
	TUE	27	MUNICH, Nachtwerk
	WED BERLIN		
	THU	29	BERLIN, Lott
	FRI	30	HAMBURG, Markthalle
DECEMBER	SAT	1	COPENHAGEN, Barbue
	SUN	2	STOCKHOLM, New Melody

Fair Warning (Agency) Limited
The Plaza, 535 Kings Road, London SW10 0SZ. Telephone: 071-376 8501
Fax: 071-376 8336. Telex: 21029 JACKOS G.

Directors: J. W. Jackson (Managing) A. J. Taylor B.A., F.C.A.
Registered No. 1741200 Licence [illegible]

18 OCT '90 15:02 071 376 8336 PAGE.002

Schedule for UK and European tour, 1990.
We were stranded in Europe at the end of this tour because while we were away Pan Am had gone bankrupt and cancelled our flights home. A stressful end to a stressful tour, although we were playing well; the live recording *Copenhagen* documents what would be our last European show (Stockholm was cancelled).

above Ticket for Paris show, 1990.

below UK poster that the promoter patterned after a Velvet Underground poster.

Damon's painted bass drumhead.
Damon always played a jazz drum set. We took the bass drumhead to an old-fashioned sign painter in Boston—"Sam Stone, Man of Letters"— and asked him to paint our name on it in "big band" style.

Paris, 1989.
Photos by Renaud Monfourny.

Paris, 1990.
Photos by Renaud Monfourny.

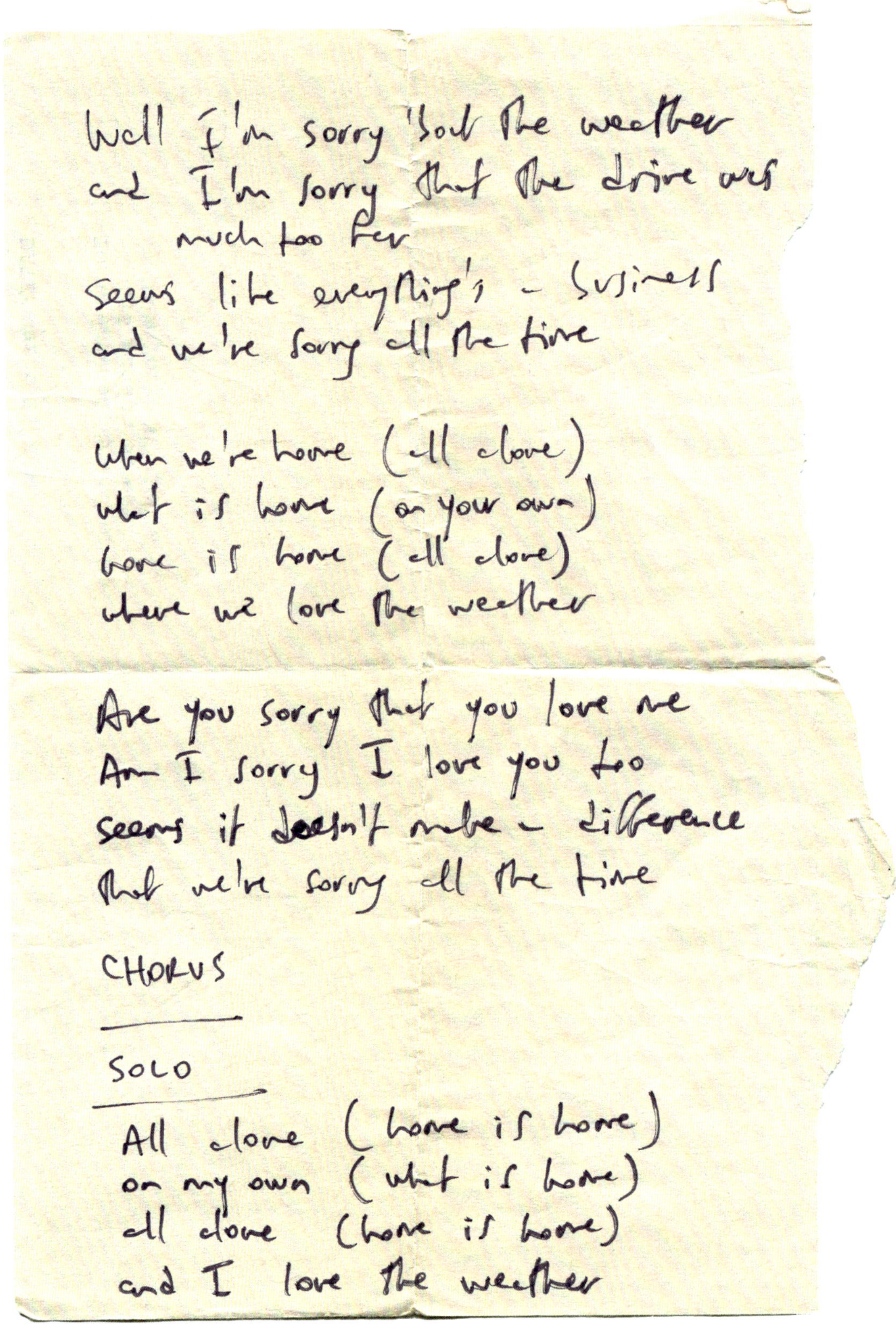

Well I'm sorry 'bout the weather
and I'm sorry that the drive was
much too far
Seems like everything's a business
and we're sorry all the time

When we're home (all alone)
what is home (on your own)
home is home (all alone)
where we love the weather

Are you sorry that you love me
Am I sorry I love you too
seems it doesn't make a difference
that we're sorry all the time

CHORUS

SOLO

All alone (home is home)
on my own (what is home)
all alone (home is home)
and I love the weather

Damon's lyrics for "Sorry" from *This is Our Music*, Summer 1990.
Maybe the only time Damon wrote lyrics for Dean to sing…

MARTIN ASTON: I knew the internal dynamics of the band: a couple and one other person is not really workable unless everyone is the same kind of person. Damon and Naomi were more homey, straightforward people; Dean was the wilder card.

DAMON KRUKOWSKI: Dean quit. Is there really more to say? The band was on the verge of moving to a major label, Columbia was the most likely candidate, and Dean quit. We'd already had our meeting at Black Rock. We'd already had our big serious meeting with our lawyer, Richard Grabel, spelling out what he expected to happen next and discussing what we wanted from the deal that was in the works. "Complete artistic control" was my mantra—I think we must have learned the phrase from Sonic Youth. Richard kept saying, after every point he ticked off on his list, so you're all agreed on that? And we'd all say yes. I guess Dean had his fingers crossed?

DEAN WAREHAM: Right after the end of our tour opening for the Cocteau Twins (I think this was Monday morning, April 8, 1991), we had played our last show at Bowdoin College on Saturday night, and I had driven back to New York the next day. I was going to call them that day to break the news that I was finished, but Damon called me first that morning—to book plane tickets for a Japanese tour. I said I didn't want to go. Isn't that how people often leave a band? Someone is informed about an upcoming gig and they say, you know what, I'm not going.

NAOMI YANG: Damon called Dean to say he was going to buy our plane tickets to Japan for the tour we had booked there, and Dean said he quit. Damon asked why and Dean said he had nothing more to say to us. I couldn't believe Dean could just throw everything away so carelessly and not even want to discuss it. I got on the phone and did something I had never done before: I yelled at him and told him he was lazy and a selfish coward. Then I hung up.

KRAMER: How many days before the Japanese tour did Dean quit the band? I was so excited to go on that, and Damon and Naomi were literally packing their bags when he told them he wasn't going. Even though they were unhappy together, I can't believe he left then; the world was ours at the time!

DAMON KRUKOWSKI: How did I feel when Dean quit? Are you kidding? Listen to *More Sad Hits!*

DEAN WAREHAM: I felt free.

TERRY TOLKIN: I wasn't surprised at all when they broke up, because I did it. I took Dean to lunch and told him that I was going to be leaving for a major label (Elektra) soon, and I just wanted him. He breathed a long sigh of relief. Dean's not that confrontational, and Galaxie 500 coulda dragged on for even another fucking album because of it.

DEAN WAREHAM: We might have been well-served by a manager who could have perhaps explained a few simple things to us. I regret that it ended badly—but that's how things often end.

NAOMI YANG: We had certainly had our share of band frictions, but we also had such a long friendship; I think I always assumed that we could always work anything out. I was so shocked and disappointed that Dean didn't even want to try. I hadn't realized how much of my identity was wrapped up in the band, in being in Galaxie 500. I felt completely stripped of my musical identity; it took a long time to recover.

DAmon

GALAXIE 500

support for Cocteau Twins tour
MARCH 12, 1991
to
APRIL 03, 1991

Tues.	MARCH 12	AMERICAN THEATRE	ST. LOUIS,MO.
WED .	MARCH 13	OFF	HOUSTON,TX.
Thu.	MARCH 14	AVALON BALLROOM	HOUSTON,TX.
Fri.	MARCH 15	METROPLEX ARENA	DALLAS,TX.
Sat.	MARCH 16	OFF	LOS ANGELES,CA.
Sun.	MARCH 17	OFF	LOS ANGELES,CA.
Mon.	MARCH 18	BREN CENTER/UCLA	IRVINE,CA.
Tue.	MARCH 19	WARFIELD THEATRE	SAN FRANCISCO,CA.
Wed.	MARCH 20	WARFIELD THEATRE	SAN FRANCISCO,CA.
Thu.	MARCH 21	OFF	SAN FRANCISCO,CA.
Fri.	MARCH 22	ORPHEUM THEATRE	VANCOUVER,B.C.
Sat.	MARCH 23	PARAMOUNT THEATRE	SEATTLE,WA.
Sun.	MARCH 24	OFF	SEATTLE,WA.
Mon.	MARCH 25	OFF	SEATTLE,WA.
Tue.	MARCH 26	PARAMOUNT THEATRE	DENVER,CO.
Wed.	MARCH 27	OFF	CHICAGO,IL.
Thu.	MARCH 28	RIVIERA THEATRE	CHICAGO,IL.
Fri.	MARCH 29	MICHIGAN THEATRE	ANN ARBOR,MI.
Sat.	MARCH 30	PALACE THEATRE	COLUMBUS,OH.
Sun.	MARCH 31	OFF	BALTIMORE,MD.
Mon.	APRIL 01	PAINTERS MILL	BALTIMORE,MD.
Tue.	APRIL 02	ROSELAND BALLROOM	NEW YORK,N.Y.
Wed.	APRIL 03	WALT. BROWN ARENA/B.U.	BOSTON,MA.

Tour schedule opening for Cocteau Twins in the US, Spring 1991.
The last Galaxie 500 tour.

WHEN - HOME
FLOWERS
SUMMERTIME
SORRY
FOURTH OF JULY
MELT AWAY
YONO

Setlist, backstage passes, and a photo I took of Robin Guthrie with his daughter, 1991.

CONTRACT

This contract for the personal services of musicians on the date below is made between the undersigned promoter and the undersigned agent for musicians on this 8th day of March 1991

Band: Galaxie 500

Name, Address & Phone number of venue: Moulton Union Main Lounge
Bowdoin College. One College Street. Brunswick, ME 04011

Date of Engagement: Friday April 5, 1991

Compensation agreed upon: $ 1,400 flat

Other: See band rider

Make payment as follows: By school check payable to Dean Wareham
Check must be given to band representative at the show

Age limit: ALL-AGES

Merchandise percentage: 0%

Admission price to venue: $ 2 for students & $ 6 general public

Capacity of venue: 200

Times: Load In: 4:00 Sound Check: 5:00 Doors open: ______
Show Begins: 9:00 On Stage: 10:00

Allowed Set Length: Band will be allowed sixty (60) minutes on stage

Billing Position: Band will receive 100% headline billing and will play last on a two (2) band bill

Promoter: Bill Fruth/Bowdoin College	Agent: Bob Lawton
Bowdoin College	TwinTowers Touring
Student Activities	611 Broadway, Suite 616
Moulton Union/ 1 College Street	New York, NY 10012
Brunswick, ME 04011	(212) 995-0649 (PH#)
(207) 725-3186	(212) 979-1428 (fax)
X ______	X ______

Contract for Bowdoin College show, Spring 1991.
This turned out to be the final Galaxie 500 show. I think about 25 people were there. Maybe fewer.

Galaxie 500 have disbanded. After returning from a successful tour of the States with Cocteau Twins, Dean unexpectedly quit the band, "to do other things," although he has no immediate plans. Damon and Naomi are "still adjusting to the news" but plan to go ahead with a side project EP scheduled for June release on Rough Trade.

Damon's fax to Rough Trade for press release of band break-up.

01/05 '91 13:56 FAX 081 880 1760 ROUGH TRADE 001

MELODY MAKER, May 4 1991

GALAXIE 500 split

GALAXIE 500 have split after guitarist/vocalist Dean Wareham quit unexpectedly. All band commitments, including a June tour of Japan, have been cancelled.

The break-up occurred when the band returned from a successful tour of the States with Cocteau Twins.

Drummer Damon Krukowski told the Maker, "One day we were planning for a tour of Japan, and the next day he just quit. It was a big surprise for me and Naomi".

According to Krukowski, Wareham left because he felt the band had "become more like a job than a hobby".

The split came at a time when Galaxie 500 were, according to Krukowski, doing well and putting more energy into their work. This success had led to Columbia approaching the band about a US distribution deal. But it seems it was this which triggered Wareham's departure.

Wareham, who had been thinking of leaving the band for some time, said: "A couple of major record labels were ready to talk to us and if I had stayed with the band, I would have to keep my plans to leave secret for a long time."

Wareham has been writing with a view to recording material with a new band. Krukowski and bassist Naomi Yang are still "in shock" and have decided to ditch the band name. In the meantime they release an EP in June on Rough Trade. It was a separate project, recorded in January at a time when Wareham wanted a "break from recording". It's titled "Pierre Etoile" and, ironically, was a comment about the pointlessness of a solo career. It features three tracks, "In The Sun", "1969" and "This Car Climbed Mount Washington".

Fax of split announcement, *Melody Maker*, Spring 1991.

Paris, 1989.
Photo by R. Deluze.

DEAN WAREHAM: Rough Trade went bankrupt in 1991, but Geoff Travis finally got his label name back in 2000 (after running a new label named Tugboat Records).

DAMON KRUKOWSKI: I don't know if you know this, but Rough Trade never accounted to Galaxie 500 for any royalties. None. And then, shortly after the band broke up, the New York office declared bankruptcy, which threw all our masters into a court auction. I went to Geoff for help, and he said, "There's nothing I can do." But there was loads he could have done, even if only provide us with the paperwork we needed to help make our case to the bankruptcy court. I ended up getting that instead from a sympathetic employee in London.

It was those documents I used to help us win our rights back at auction. I needed to convince the court that the band was owed a lot of royalties, in order to make it possible to buy the rights to our masters for an amount we could afford. I built up a claim and then waived it as a part of the offer we made. Anyone could have come in and outbid us, but they would have had to match both our (small) cash bid, plus the (large) lien I had placed against our contracts. No one did, so the band won back its rights. My father always wanted me to be a lawyer! But thank God that was my only day in court. The process took months, and I remember feeling sickened by the whole thing, more than anything. Who ever thought you could auction off band contracts? It was so perverse.

DEAN WAREHAM: We do have contact, via email. We made three albums together, and those records are our children; even though we're divorced we still need to talk about the children occasionally.

DAMON KRUKOWSKI: Dean and I email each other all the time, for business reasons. But we haven't been in the same room, or even spoken on the phone, since he quit Galaxie 500. A bit childish, no? But business-wise—here in the present—everything is OK.

NAOMI YANG: We are asked constantly about a reunion. It is either the first or last question of every interview. I just don't see any reason for it, so I doubt it will change.

DEAN WAREHAM: I think a reunion of Speedy & the Castanets is more likely.

DAMON KRUKOWSKI: For God's sake, all the rest was so long ago. So let's leave it like that. No reunion.

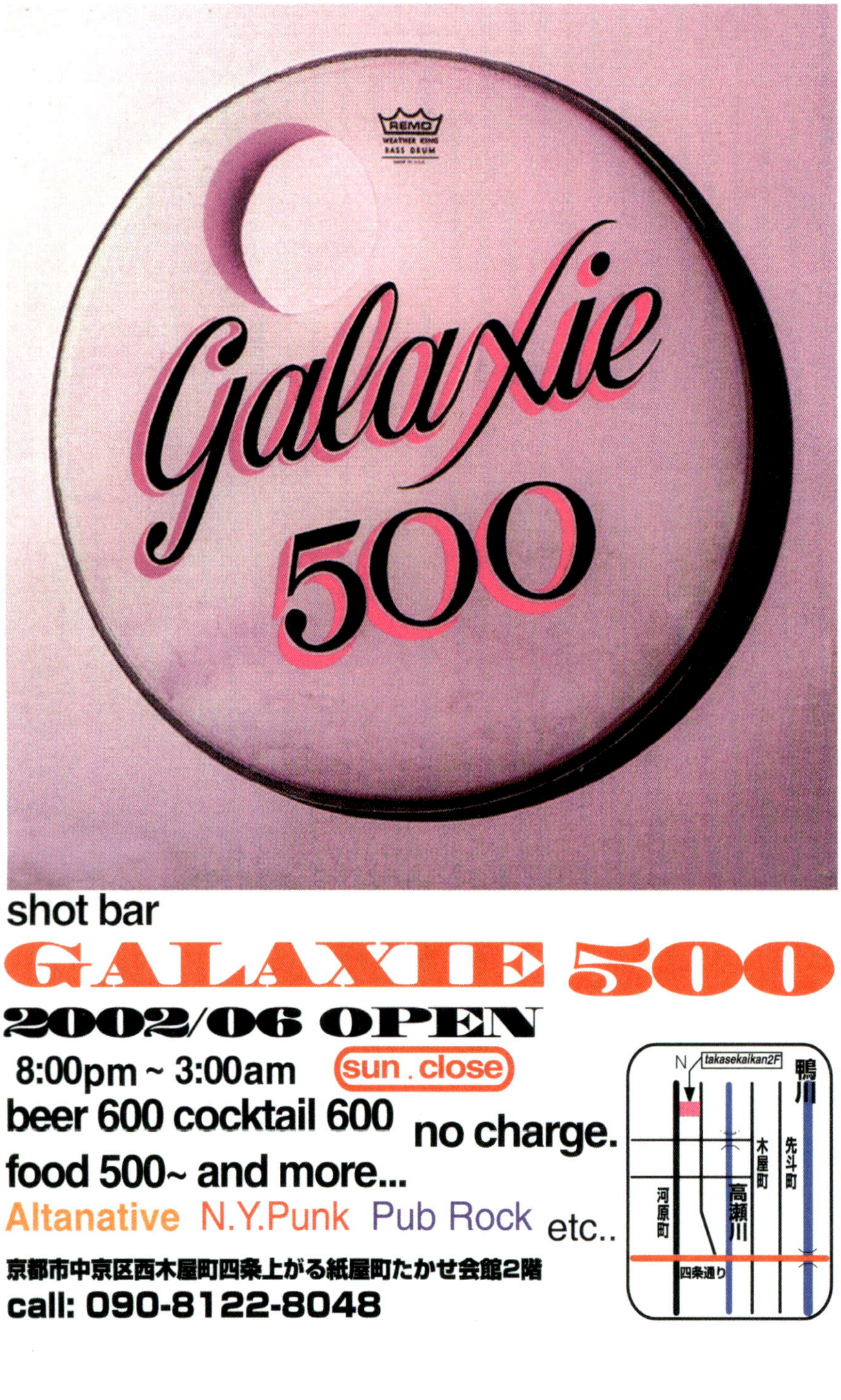

Flyer for Galaxie 500 Shot Bar, Kyoto, 2002.

Announcement for the Armory Show, New York, 2003.
Watercolor by Barnaby Furnas.

Yoshimoto Nara installation, Hara Museum of Contemporary Art, Tokyo, 2004.

14 **PICTURES**

NAOMI YANG: You asked before about regrets…I might have some typographical regrets!

I think all three of us shared a pretty sophisticated visual sense and certainly strong feelings that design was important. I was lucky in that Dean and Damon and the record companies we worked with gave me pretty much completely free rein to design whatever I wanted. I had been trained as a graphic designer/architect and so it was very natural for me to start making band posters, t-shirts, ephemera, etc.

FRANCIS DIMENNO: Their album covers made a statement: Cool Restraint. Educated. Upper Class. Lots of Social Contacts.

NAOMI YANG: I was a visual art major at Harvard; my senior thesis was in painting but I also did projects in photography, industrial design, and landscape studies. I took one class in graphic design, but otherwise it was something that I did more outside of school. I designed posters for plays and concert—even a logo for Speedy & the Castanets. At that moment in rock history, every band needed a logo!

The summer before I went to Harvard I worked as an apprentice in Milton Glaser's office in New York. In high school I had done a lot of poster design and Milton Glaser was my hero. I spent most of that summer making photostats. Back then, it was the only way you could change the size of the type that you ordered from a typesetter—otherwise you had to reorder all new type. The photostat machine was a huge camera-contraption with which you took a photo of the type, altering the percentage of the original, and then developing it inside the machine by sticking your arms through these holes and looking through a little light-safe window. And then, if you changed your mind, and decided you wanted yet a different size of type—you had to make another photostat!

BYRON COLEY: Naomi has a splendid eye, which was always one of their signatures—apart from that first single.

NAOMI YANG: I am always drawn to the simple and the well proportioned rather than the flashy. I often joke with Damon that if I started a design movement I would call it the "Plain Style."

The original artwork was all derived from what I could do with a Xerox machine—cut-up, collaged, and tailored to what would reproduce well in very high-contrast black and white. Later, when we were able to use offset printing, I had a chance to experiment with color and use photography in a more subtle way.

When we started, I loved the Factory Records graphic design and typography of Peter Saville just as I loved the bass playing of Peter Hook—the two were sort of intertwined in my mind. I also admired the Blue Note album covers, both for the typography as well as the beautiful photography. I was also influenced by the poetic, dream-like, associative nature of Milton Glaser's work. As I grew more experienced in design, I was able to move away from the safety of symmetry in the first covers and became more confident about using asymmetry on the page, and different proportions.

DEAN WAREHAM: Naomi came up with the design ideas, and executed them. And I think it was a very important part of our appeal. I think using the Atget photograph on the cover of *Today* was brilliant.

NAOMI YANG: My father was a photographer who loved Eugene Atget, so I grew up being very familiar with Atget's work. I felt like the photo of the rose garden captured the ephemeral mood of an album called *Today*. Later, I started using my own photographs as cover illustrations, but the *Today* cover is a perfect synthesis of all my deep visual influences at that point in time.

FRANCIS DIMENNO: I never thought about it much until now, but of course from this vantage point it seems perfectly obvious that they were using simplicity in graphic design to make a statement. That less is more.

NAOMI YANG: I had originally wanted to be a painter, and when I dropped out of architecture school it was to paint as well as play music. But Galaxie 500 was doing so well that I had no time to paint, and I felt worried that I wasn't really spending my time making art—it was pop culture, and somehow a much less valuable pursuit than painting. I suffered a lot of anxiety about that as we toured and spent all our time on music—that I was not attending to the real art that I hoped to make. Graphic design certainly posed a similar problem to me. It was fun, like music, not solitary and miserable, like painting, and therefore not as worthy.

DAMON KRUKOWSKI. We actually wrote design control into our contract with Rough Trade, even specifying how many colors Naomi would be allowed to use on the album covers.

NAOMI YANG: I can't quite separate the design of anything for Galaxie 500 from how I was feeling about the music and the band at the time. I think I feel happiest with the *Blue Thunder* EP. I was very proud of the photograph I had taken in a park in Paris, and I think the metallic inks printed beautifully, just as I wanted. And the typography was successful. It very strongly mimics the form of a Blue Note album cover, but I really had fun faking one. And that was a particularly happy and optimistic time in the band.

DAMON KRUKOWSKI: We had to teach our lawyer, Richard Grabel, the term "Pantone" so he could add it in. He got into it, I think because he was amused by the idea; he said he didn't know of anyone else who had ever put printing specs into their record contract.

NAOMI YANG: At the point [of designing the second album], I had come to really love and appreciate Elektra covers from the late '60s and early '70s—those iconic band photos, the band outdoors, often backlit, or photographed from a dramatic angle. I had this very clearly in mind, so I wanted to take the photo myself. I scouted for a good location and found it at Harvard's Arnold Arboretum, on a hill in an orchard. On the day of the shoot, I set up my camera with a cable release, and positioned us with me in the middle so that I could look through the lens, framing Damon and Dean to make sure that everyone was in the shot, and then run around to be in it too. I am bending over in the photo and pressing the shutter release. The cover typeface was very special; I ordered it from Dan X. Solo, a typographer in San Francisco who specialized in old display type, like the ones used on rock posters in the '60s.

MARTIN ASTON: They had a vision which extended to the design. But it was Naomi's thing (and Damon's too). I don't know whether Dean had much input. I guess he would have had the power of veto, but I never asked.

NAOMI YANG: Looking back, I think the choice of typeface on *This Is Our Music* is really a rather strange one. At the time it seemed so cool to me, kind of retro '70s, but in hindsight it seems pretty clumsy. I also remember showing Geoff Travis my mock-up for the cover. I thought the photos (which I still think are beautiful portraits of each of us) were very stylish but I was worried they were too slick. I asked him if he thought they were too "commercial" and he said, "I think they are rather sinister." Now I look at them and think how interesting it is that I chose to use individual portraits of each of us as the band was falling apart; maybe a group photo at that moment was emotionally not possible?

Imaginary comic book cover by Tavi Gevinson, editor of *Rookie*, 2011.

MIKE McGONIGAL: I was lucky to have been sent their first 7" in the mail for review. I excitedly called up their label head, Marc Alghini, and we became fast friends. I played that little blue record so many times it started to sound fuzzy. The group gave me a song from their first recording sessions which I released on a 7" compilation with the fanzine I published out of the row house in Queens that I lived in.

I put on two shows they performed at, something I rarely do because it's such a pain in the ass. But with Galaxie, I really just wanted to make sure I got to see them as often as possible. They were a tremendously exciting live band, and I'm not sure how well this has been captured, but they were capable of getting very loud when they wanted to. There was a fabulous little show at a yoga studio on the Lower East Side with the Go Team and Mecca Normal. I remember encouraging them to play "Here She Comes Now" for the encore. Afterwards I fought with Calvin Johnson and Tobi Vail over what qualified as acceptable dance music (they did not want to hear the Shaggs as such). Paleface wrote a fun song about the show, "Galaxie 500 Party Song." Then there was a super-packed benefit at CBGB for the tiny basement-level fanzine shop I worked at then, See Hear. Its entire inventory had been destroyed by mysterious flooding.

Sonic Youth and B.A.L.L. also played the benefit. I was surprised that Sonic Youth liked Galaxie so much; they seemed to come from totally different worlds. At the time, I knew the band fairly well and hung around the studio when their second record was made. I didn't realize myself that they were unhappy with each other until way late. After he moved back to New York to be near his pretty actor girlfriend, Dean lent me $500 to help get an issue of my fanzine out. It had a compilation 7" with a solo Dean track, his four-tracked cover of a Beat Happening song (which Sonic Boom later recorded himself, unaware it was a cover).

While preparing this little volume—an early version of which ran originally as a multi-volume article for the online magazine *Pitchfork*—I read in a review of *Uncollected* that Galaxie 500 was "largely undiscovered in their day." And their bio on *All Music Guide* leads off that band was "criminally overlooked in their own lifetime." This is news to me. And heaven knows what these people would say about actually obscure and overlooked Boston-area acts like the Girls, Ed's Redeeming Qualities or High Risk Group.

Galaxie 500 was a really well-regarded indie-rock band at the time; they were a perfect date band, as your girl was as bound to like them as much as you (this was, and is, very important). They signed to a big indie label, they got to tour a lot, to record with the single producer on Earth they were most suited to work with, and they were absolutely adored over in Europe.

Galaxie 500 made three great records that people bought thousands of copies of, then broke up before they could suck. What more could you want? When Liz Phair's "Girly Sound" tapes started to circulate around the time of Galaxie's third album, it was no surprise to hear her sing on "Stratford-On-Guy," "I was pretending that I was in a Galaxie 500 video." Heck, we'd already done the same thing ourselves, more than once.

NAOMI YANG: Looking back at the ephemera in this book, I am kind of amazed at the things I saved; I guess I have a bit of an archivist's instinct in me. These scraps of paper with bits of thoughts jotted down on them, the letters, the receipts and the postcards were all written in a time before personal computers and before email—they must have seemed artifacts worth preserving—the physical evidence of what I was experiencing during that time, separate from the music.

In 1996, when the Galaxie 500 Box Set was released by Rykodisc, it was only five years after the band had broken up. The Box Set came out in the fall, and after having worked on the release for the better part of the year, I told Damon I had the desire to throw one off a bridge into the Charles River on New Year's Eve—to symbolically free us from the past. (In the end I realized the river would probably be frozen and it would just land with an unsatisfying thud, so I didn't do it.)

Now, over 20 years after Galaxie 500 broke up, I look through these pages with quite a different feeling: less of loss and more a mixture of nostalgia and the shock of how long ago it really all was, of how much our world, and I—as artist and musician and person—have changed in the time since. I am grateful for not having let my youth go to waste and I am looking forward to adventures to come.